THE ART OF
NOT DOING

HOW TO ACHIEVE INNER PEACE
AND A CLEAR MIND

ANDREW GEORGE MARSHALL

RADIANT SUN BOOKS
STAFFORD, ENGLAND

Radiant Sun Books
30 Haywood Grange
Little Haywood, Stafford ST18 0UB
www.radiantsunbooks.com

Book Layout ©2013 BookDesignTemplates.com

Cover design by Sarah-Jane Lehoux

The Art of Not Doing/ Andrew Marshall – 1st ed.
ISBN 978-0-9559364-9-4

CONTENTS

To all my teachers – past, present and future

Do not look for a sanctuary in anyone but yourself

Siddhartha Gautama

What this book can do for you

THE WORLD IS FAST; life is fast. This is good and exciting, right?

Well, up to a point. The trouble is that inside we are going round at high speed, too. Our minds don't know how to stop. And the body suffers as we put it under increasing levels of tension and stress. Life may be exciting but we don't have time to be happy – and maybe we won't always have time to be healthy either.

Ok – so we can learn to relax. This is good. But it doesn't cure the problem. It's just a sticking plaster – a temporary fix that we apply through some relaxation technique. Then we go back into activity – back onto the spinning carousel.

In this book you will learn much more than relaxation. You will discover not only why the mind craves incessant activity, but how to break the cycle by applying the universal law of cause and effect. You will learn how to rediscover the natural deep peace that lies within you and how to look at the world through different eyes.

Through cultivating inner peace, we can lead a stress-free life; but there is much more to be had from life than being free of stress. Learning how to look deeply, we can access more creative and intuitive levels of mind. And by living fully in the present moment, we develop a real presence – a presence that comes naturally when we have learned how to stop and be who we really are.

Meditation techniques can help us benefit from our internal energy or *chi*. Chi has the capacity to revitalise the body and also to lead to extraordinarily clear states of mind or consciousness.

But this is not a book about mere introspection. *The Art of Not Doing* is about balance – becoming skilled at balancing our outer life of activity with our inner, and our innermost, aspects. In touch with our own essence or spirit, we truly enter the stream of life and allow our full potential to be realised.

And we can begin this very moment...

[1]

Not doing

OUR HABITUAL LOSS OF AWARENESS

WITHOUT REALISING IT, all of us lose our awareness every day. We may not be asleep but it is as though we are dreaming, making our way through life without full consciousness of the present moment and of who we really are. In a dream, the craziest things seem real. On waking, that reality dissolves into the mists of illusion. Now, we take life to be real because we think we are awake but, as we shall see, we are not fully awake. Knowing who we are has nothing to do with our name, our family, education, work or anything else. In fact, it is those things, amongst others, that we get lost in – temporary images of who we think, or assume, we are.

Our problem lies in our tendency to react to life's events with only *partial* awareness. It is a habit that has been with us since we were born. In a sense, we are half asleep. Only part of our being is engaged in what we do. If we are travelling to work, for example, all sorts of things may engage our mind. The main one will be to reach our destination, to be at a specific juncture of space and time – our place of work – at a set hour. Any obstruction or delay on the journey may frustrate us and lead to a mishmash of thoughts and feelings. As the journey progresses, the mind will probably wander to the events of the day and possibly to those of the past; we may also think from time to time of longer-range projects. For many of us, most of the time, a journey is only about the destination – literally a means to an end – and the same applies to so many of our activities. They are not a source of enjoyment in themselves because the mind is elsewhere, yet they could be if the awareness were settled and clear.

Throughout our waking hours, the mind is incessantly wandering, causing fluctuations of energy in the body. When a positive thought occurs, it is usually accompanied by a pleasant feeling together with an increase in energy; conversely, when an unhappy flow of thoughts comes, the feeling is not so good and our mood and sense of well-being take a nosedive.[1] These changes nudge the next stream of thoughts into either a positive or negative direction; and if we don't like the feeling our thoughts generate, we will often tend to look for a distraction that is temporarily more pleasant.

---

[1] Research at Ohio University found that negative thinking can have a detrimental effect on the body as it increases levels of inflammation through the production of C-reactive protein. – Dr Peggy Zoccola, Assistant Professor of Psychology (reported by the Office of Research Communications, Ohio University, March 13, 2013).

Distractions can prevent us falling into an abyss but they can also help us to avoid facing up to the real matters in life that we need to deal with. A little diversion can be very useful and positive, of course. If we are suffering from illness, injury or grief, it can be therapeutic to engage in some activity or other form of distraction so that the focus is taken away from pain and discomfort, allowing the body's natural healing processes to continue. But the meandering mind takes our vitality with it and during much of the day our energy is needlessly dissipated.

The mind puts itself into an almost perpetual state of motion. By and large, our mind is not used to being in a state of "not doing". It will engage itself in almost anything, so long as it doesn't have to stop and become aware of itself. Perhaps we are afraid of stopping because if there is nothing to think about and nothing to focus on, what is left? Most of us have a fear of the unknown and of having nothing to cling on to, so we busy ourselves in the practice of chronic avoidance. As we shall see later, however, there is nothing whatsoever to be fearful about. In fact, all fears disappear once we know who we are.

Our habitual patterns of reaction are greatly conditioned by the self-identity we have each created – the "I" and "me" that underlies, qualifies and colours everything we think, say and do. We label ourselves according to our name, occupation, upbringing, likes, dislikes, relationships and so on. "Me" is a concept we have created – a mentally constructed "object" – that resides in the space of our awareness. Identifying ourselves with that object, we distinguish everything else as being separate from us. The Art of Not Doing is a skill in re-establishing a truer sense of self-identity and becoming more conscious of our wonderful inner space of awareness. As that develops, the dominance of "me" gradually wanes, so that we identify with the whole, rather than seeing ourselves as an entity separate from it. Until that view dawns, the mind engages itself with thoughts, feelings and ideas (which we can call *internal objects*) and with appearances and forms (*external objects*).

The Art of Not Doing is about freeing ourselves from our addiction to objects, both internal and external, and in doing so becoming more aware of space. Whatever the mind is occupied with, there is always an object of focus. If we look around wherever we are right now, we will see objects. If we are in a room, there will be furniture, walls, ceiling, flooring and fittings; there may be other people around. If we were asked to describe our surroundings, we would probably refer to what we can see, rather than what we can't see. Yet it is space that governs the relationship between objects and, indeed, between ourselves and others. But what we see through the eyes is only part of the picture. For the mind constructs images and impressions from internal signals that are as real as those that originate from the five senses. For this very reason, some Eastern schools of philosophy refer to the mind as the sixth sense. Simply closing the eyes so that the world disappears from view for a short while is not the answer. Somehow, we need to increase our ability to be aware not only of objects – both internal and external – that demand our attention, but also the space in which they appear. We then need to be able to hold that experience with total clarity.

In today's world, it is very difficult to be clear. Minds work more rapidly than they ever have. Communications are fast, if not instantaneous, and are so numerous we cannot possibly hope to cope with them all. Every day, we are bombarded with stimuli – advertising, emails, text messages, telephone calls, junk mail, television, internet and so on. We are kept so busy, our minds never have time to settle. Indeed, we are so skilled at leaping to new matters of fleeting interest that we have largely lost the skill to remain with one. To advance in that skill, we have to learn how to stop.

THE VALUE OF STOPPING

How often do we actually stop and do nothing? Even if we are given an opportunity to sit down and take a break, there's a good chance that we will look for something to do. Perhaps we might pick up a magazine or a book, check our emails, send a text or do a puzzle. If we try to sit and do nothing, we will probably end up thinking about something. Rarely do we allow the mind and body to become still. The mind is like a wheel that is always spinning. If we want the mind to slow down, we have to stop feeding it and allow the continual streams of thoughts to come to rest. Out of habit, we keep it going, and yet we need to train the mind to become slower and clearer. When the mind is whirling from one thing to another, it seems impossible to do anything about it. But we can – and we must if we want to reconnect with our true state of being.

If we don't learn to stop for ourselves, nature can force us to take a break. When we are extremely busy over a long period of time and there is no let-up in pressure, the body's stress responses are much greater. We actually wear the body out much faster when we are stressed. The immune system weakens[2] and the blood pressure increases. Often, sleep patterns deteriorate and we become tired. But because we get used to that level of fatigue and to the loss of well-being that comes with it, we carry on. It's almost as though the winds of life are passing through us so quickly that they begin to wear us out. We're familiar with the effects of wind or water erosion – this is erosion due to *internal* elements. And then something gives way. The body falls ill – perhaps just a cold or maybe something more serious. Either way, life is saying, "Just a moment..." and we are forced to stop, or at least to slow down, so that the body can begin to recover.

And yet stopping is more than a matter of preserving health. A pause gives us time to breathe and to appreciate everything we have. When we appreciate and feel grateful for life, we value and respect ourselves and others. Rushing around prevents us from appreciating anything, as does trying to do many things at once or thinking about one thing whilst doing another. For example, many people do not enjoy the food they eat because their minds are on other things – television, reading or whatever they are going to do next. Quite unwittingly, they deny themselves the oppor-

---

[2] See, for example, Patrick Bouic PhD & Lorna Vanderhaeghe, *The Immune System Cure*, (New York 1999).

tunity for a deep appreciation of what they have, what they are engaged in – and, indeed, of themselves. As a result, eating becomes a mere mechanical activity and a common result is poor or inappropriate diet. Fast food often means fast intake – and the same principle applies to anything in life. It really is difficult to enjoy the scenery when we are speeding along.

Knowing who and what we are is impossible when the mind is lost in thoughts and emotions. Some might say, "Does it really matter?" After all, to know oneself sounds a bit philosophical and dry. Knowing oneself, however, is not a matter of theory or intellectual understanding but of direct experience. When we have glimpses of that experience, we begin the process of self-realisation which is the most important thing we can do – fulfilling our evolutionary purpose. It is a matter of losing our false sense of identity and becoming true to ourselves and to the world. We are rewarded with inner peace and happiness and a sense of relief because we discover there is nothing that we need to cling on to.

A simple thing we can do at any time of the day is to stop what we are doing. Then listen and be aware of what is going on, particularly in the mind. Does the mind come to a state of quietness easily or is it distracted? Is the breathing quiet or erratic? Is remaining in this state for a few minutes easy or does the mind urge us to go back into activity? Do we feel happy and content?

The answers to these questions can give us some indication of the stillness or lack of it within us. The more inner activity there is going on, the stronger the currents in our emotional and mental streams of energy (sometimes called winds) within our system. Most of the time, we are not even aware of these winds but just react without thinking. If we can make ourselves aware of them, we are already taking a small step towards the experience of self-knowledge.

We may think that inner stillness can only come from attending meditation retreats or withdrawing from normal life. That if we lead a busy life with all its attendant responsibilities, such a luxury is not a viable option, even if we desire it.[3] However, it is much more beneficial, as well as more practical, to undertake some simple meditation exercises to bring about tranquillity and a clearer awareness whilst partaking in a normal lifestyle. That way, the positive effects of our practice stabilise much more quickly than if we move from an artificial environment back to a busy one. For the vast majority, everyday life actually provides more than enough opportunity for practice.

Giving ourselves room to pause and breathe isn't just a case of following formal or structured practices. Art, for example, can play an important role in helping us to enjoy a temporary break in the ceaseless chain of thoughts from which we all suffer. By engaging the awareness, art can help the mind transcend its normal patterns. Just gazing and admiring a picture or a sculpture, for example, without try-

---

[3] Even under such special conditions, clarity and stillness do not come easily. Some Eastern meditation teachers have been known to shock their students out of reverie by making a loud noise or even striking them. Occasionally that can bring an instantaneous recognition of pure awareness – but that is not a method to use at home!

ing to analyse or judge it in any way, can be enormously soothing and uplifting. And of course, the greatest sculptor and painter is nature herself. There is plenty in our environment to help us pause and disengage for a while; we only have to look.

WHY BEING IS MORE IMPORTANT THAN DOING

The Art of Not Doing is not about cultivating a lifestyle with a complete absence of activity. Learning to stop is a crucial part of it but we also have to develop an enhanced level of awareness. It's about reaching what might be called a state of *super-charged consciousness*, one that goes beyond our normal realms of activity into a perception of what is sometimes known as the *ground of our being*.

If we live just for the next thing we are going to do, or maybe the next hundred things on our list of things we must accomplish, it is very difficult to maintain a conscious connection with our being. Our connection is probably at best with our schedule or possibly the task in hand; at worst, our consciousness will be lost in myriad thoughts, fears and other mental and emotional detritus. Awareness of *Being*, the space in which all our experiences take place, is usually absent.

It is said in some traditional teachings[4] that awareness and Being are inseparable and that it can be helpful to think

---

[4] For example, the Dzogchen and Mahamudra teachings of Tibetan Buddhism. See Chökyi Nyima Rinpoche, *The Union of Mahamudra & Dzogchen* (Hong Kong 1994).

of the unity of awareness and Being as having similar characteristics to space. More than space, however, Being has the ability or potential to know and to experience. Being is not inert; it is cognisant. Everything we perceive through the mind and the senses arises within the ground of being. Because Being is beyond any concept, it is very difficult to understand and the mind will try to compare it with things we are familiar with. That is why knowledge of Being can only come through experience; intellectual arguments can only discriminate or distinguish, and so we come across statements such as, "it is not like this and it is not like that," or "it is neither this nor that." This is rather like trying to describe the taste of a strawberry to someone who had never eaten one; it's impossible to convey the experience to another person. Although we may be able to describe its appearance, we can only say what the strawberry doesn't taste like by comparing it to other flavours; even words such as sweet and sour are comparative terms. The experience of Being transcends language completely.

In spite of the inadequacy of words to describe it, the experience of Being is not some distant phenomenon. Being is our ever-present nature – but whose presence has become a vague, distant memory. We are like actors in a play who have become so lost in their parts, or children who have become so engrossed in their games, that they have forgotten who they really are.

We take life for granted without having regard to the whole. Our individual lives are tiny particles or foci within the grand space of the whole cosmos, but we are unlikely to give much thought to the universe when we are putting our dinner in the oven. Fortunately, though, realisation of Being does not require an awareness of solar systems or galaxies but simply an awareness of ourselves – our *whole* selves – in whatever we are doing. Awareness of Being requires a shift in focus that is simplicity itself and yet, because that shift is so simple, it is extraordinarily difficult to execute. Until we succeed in doing so, we inevitably continue to lead lives that are shrouded in the mists of not knowing and are incomplete – but cultivating this awareness can be done and is within our grasp.

While we continue to run around with thought only for things that we deem necessary or urgent but often aren't, we are missing a vital point – who is the doer of all these actions? How can we validly undertake our various tasks without knowing who we are? If we don't know who we are, then our activity, and more importantly the thoughts and beliefs that lead to them, are based on a false premise. We are in fact operating with a case of mistaken identity. We have assumed a limited notion of ourselves – name, occupation, upbringing, education, sex, nationality etc. – taking this to be the truth. Accordingly, we categorise, judge and label everything we see, hear and feel in the light of that. So our picture of the world is based on ignorant concepts and is inevitably false.

The Art of Not Doing does not mean sitting and gazing into space. It means allowing ourselves the opportunity to experience life fully by learning to be. In essence, we have to train our minds to expand so that they embrace our whole being; then we can undertake any activity without sinking back into a false self-identity. That type of expansion is no small undertaking, but a project of stupendous proportions. Our consciousness has to be refined and broadened until it becomes boundless and pure. Expansion can only occur as the ego – the sense of "I, me and mine" – shrinks. It is the ego that creates the things to do on the "unnecessary list". Our Art is a skill and, as we begin to acquire it, expectations, disappointments, worries and fears rapidly diminish, giving way to total peace of mind.

If we believe that our busy lives are of indispensable benefit to the world, it suggests that we have a lack of inner peace. Nobody is indispensable. But there are two questions we can ask ourselves that can help indicate whether our actions have real value:

> *Are my thoughts, words and actions in some way helping to make the world a better and happier place?*
>
> *Are they helping to make me a better and happier person?*

If the answer to both is no, it almost certainly means that there is a great deal more we can achieve – not by doing *more* things but by improving *how* we approach what we already do. There is an old saying that doing less can actually accomplish more. Sooner or later, we need to take that to heart.

EVOLUTION OF CONSCIOUSNESS

The nature of life is to evolve. The universe, and every form of life in it, is changing. We can think of the universe as a giant organism, in which everything has purpose. If it doesn't, it has to change or is eventually made redundant. Evolution applies not only in terms of growth and adaptation of physical forms, but to every level of life – including the most subtle or spiritual aspects – and consciousness.

The development of our own consciousness is of utmost importance in the evolutionary process because the quality of our lives and of what we think, do and say is governed by our state of consciousness. Whether we are happy or sad, angry or peaceful, isn't determined by outer circumstances but by our state of mind. Our various emotional states arise from a mixture of perceptions, beliefs and memory, aspects of our mental faculties that clearly have to change, otherwise we will continue to go round and round, like hamsters on the proverbial wheel. If we have ever had a clear experience, whether in meditation or otherwise, we know beyond any shadow of doubt that our normal ways of thinking, and everything that conditions our thinking processes, is wrong. That realisation occurs because suddenly we have a wider view. We are like a valley dweller who one day climbs to the top of a mountain and sees for the first time that there are other valleys, and indeed a different world, beyond his own.

Refinement of consciousness, and its evolution, depends on more than a single moment of clarity, though. It is a common mistake is to think that such an event is extraordinarily special and that we have attained instant enlightenment. If only that were the case! The beauty of a moment of clarity is that it can help us to question our values and our normal perceptions. Although a very long time may pass before we experience such a moment again, those precious seconds or minutes can give us the encouragement and confidence to carry on because we have a taste of what refinement of consciousness might be about. The hard work is establishing that as a normal state.

It would be wrong to think that the Art of Not Doing is simply a question of clarifying our awareness and coming to a very pleasant mental and emotional condition. There is a gradual process that involves, among other things, refinement of the brain and the nervous system because the body has to be able to support a different state of consciousness. The mind has to be trained to think in a more enlightened way, from being dominated by desires and fears into being driven by selflessness, compassion, love and confidence. Ethics play a very important part in the development process. A fully aware person is deeply sensitive to the needs and sufferings of others and is driven to act in the best possible way for the rest of humanity. Having nothing to do in the theme in this book really means not needing to do anything for oneself because one's consciousness has evolved to the point where individuality – the sense of "I, me and mine" – has been superseded by identification with the whole.

Spirituality is about the journey towards a complete realisation of who and what we really are. It has nothing to do with wishful thinking or with ideals. Experience is the key and no matter how much we analyse or philosophise, intellectual examination on its own will not bring us to it. We will just continue on a never-ending spiral of thought. At some point, thinking has to be transcended because thoughts are finite. Our true nature, as we learn once we rediscover it, is infinite – boundless and unquantifiable.

[2]

Karma

THE UNIVERSAL LAW OF CAUSE AND EFFECT

EVERYTHING IN THE AMAZING interplay of energy we call the universe is subject to an immutable principle – that every phenomenon has a preceding cause. The law of cause and effect, sometimes called the law of *karma*, particularly when applied to conduct, is an inevitable product of our three-dimensional existence. Every event occurs at a juncture of time and space and, whether great or small, creates a consequence or a series of consequences.

That we are here at all now is due to our parents at some time in the past having been initially attracted to each other and having had sex when conception was possible. Every human being on the face of the planet is here as a result of sex; all our ancestors since the beginning of humanity have only appeared, and caused their offspring to appear, as a result of the union of male and female. This is only one chain of causation.

Our planet only in exists because it is part of the solar system, itself the result of an accumulation of events that science makes intelligent guesses at understanding but cannot be absolutely certain of. However, what is clear is that without the sun, the planets would not have formed and there would be no solar system; and within it, Earth seems to us to be unique because it maintains life in forms that have not been discovered elsewhere. Its ecosystem is a wonderful example of the working out of cause and effect as nature shapes our lives and everything around us. Humanity tries to work with nature, or to get the most out of it by exploitation. With the co-operative approach, positive effects tend to be created whereas with the latter, the effects are often damaging in the longer term.

The simplest application of this general law of action and reaction is that of *immediate effect*. One identifiable event is followed by another that is directly linked to it. But there is more to the law of karma than a simple working out of preceding causes – events don't necessarily occur because something else happened just a few moments ago. Often the chain of causation is extremely complex, with lines of action coming from many directions in space and time. If we are walking along the street and walk into a lamp post, we can say that the main and obvious cause is that we were walking along without looking where we were going. Slightly more complex are the reasons why we were on that street at that particular time, why we lost our awareness (tiredness, perhaps, or a distraction) and that at some point in history, it was decided to put a lamp post right there in that particular spot which was later to coincide with our lack of attention. All the events in our lives, as well as all the manifestations and machinations of nature in its various kingdoms, are not the result of pure chance, but depend on other circumstances having occurred in the past.

That past does not have to be recent. For example, a plant may shed its seed now but the seed can remain dormant for many seasons before beginning to germinate. So it is with many occurrences – the cause cannot be pinpointed because it lies so far back in time that it is difficult to trace. Many things in our world, let alone the rest of the universe, are a mystery, but they are only inexplicable to us because the lines of causation are beyond our present knowledge and understanding.

It is crucial to understand something of cause and effect because it is of major significance to our own development. For our consciousness to evolve – the process of enlightenment or spiritual growth – there have to be the causes that allow this to happen. By and large, we have to create those causes ourselves. Acting and speaking ethically, cultivating kindness and other positive qualities that strengthen our character are examples of this. We also have to have the determination to avoid doing and saying things that have negative effects. But at times, we may become discouraged. Perhaps it seems as though everything in life is going against us and that every possible obstacle to growth is being put in our way, no matter what we do. The law of karma seems to work for us sometimes and against us at others. In actual fact, it works neither for nor against us; it simply is. When difficulties come, the important thing is to keep sowing positive seeds and trust that the evolutionary path will take us onward and upward, as it will.

KARMA – THE CONSEQUENCES OF BEHAVIOUR

Every action generates karma.[5] Nothing is without a consequence, so what we do is important because it carries the seed of the future. The practice of "not doing" doesn't mean leading a life without action but it does suggest that in order to have a calm and clear mind, whatever actions we undertake need to be carried out with care. When our conduct is not accompanied by full awareness or mindfulness, we risk creating problems that occur either immediately or sometime in the future.

Ideally, our activity should create positive seeds for the future. There are a number of ways of looking at this. A positive consequence is that the result of the act will benefit others; but we must also take great care to see that no harm is done to those who are outside the range of beneficiaries. For example, if we steal in order to provide material benefits for our family, a narrow view might cause us to think that that's all right; a more intelligent view is that although the act is done for the sake of others, some harm is being done to the victims. That is an obvious example but in the

---

[5] The word *karma* is from Sanskrit and means action, but its popular usage, which is used here, is to describe the result of action.

world of human affairs there are limitless variations on that theme, some of them so subtle that we may not perceive them as negative. The ego – our sense of "I" – conditions the way we see and how we react to events and circumstances. Even if we have made significant progress in reducing the ego, inevitably it will still colour many things whilst a trace of self-interest remains. So sometimes we may find we are guarding our own interests, being more concerned for ourselves than perhaps we are for others. It is human nature to do that and naturally we do our best to protect our home, money and resources as well as our loved ones. If that causes no harm to anyone else, all is well and good – but what if, in protecting our own concerns, we cause or prolong the unhappiness or suffering of others? Then the actions or omissions are not right because, along with the immediate positive consequences for ourselves, we have also sown negative seeds.

Karma – the results of action – applies to us as individuals and can also be accumulated by a group, a nation or a race. Collective karma is something over which we have limited control, if we have any at all. For example, if a country has benefitted through exploitation, it will also have accrued negative consequences; and the nature of karma being what it is, the negative results may not be delivered for a long time – perhaps generations later. As a race, humanity through its industrialised nations has caused damage to the environment through over-extraction of natural resources and pollution. For a while now, the consequences have begun to bite and, albeit slowly, the world has been waking up to the need to change direction. Much, much more needs to be done to put things right, of course, but it is instructive to notice how the law of cause and effect has a purpose – to guide us back into the stream of life. It is also useful to observe how collective karma affects those who have done nothing to create them. Many poorer societies are suffering the results of others' exploits whilst themselves trying to live in tune with nature.

As individuals, we shape our own future by our own actions. Although we can never know what life will throw at us, what we do today will almost certainly affect the future. Some things are more obvious than others, such as abusing the body through an unbalanced diet, too little or too much exercise, and so on. And we know, too, that if we act or speak violently, the results can be devastating. However, it is the more subtle factors that usually provide the greatest challenge. Our concern should be to identify any tendencies to negativity in our speech and actions and to winkle them out.

If we want to achieve self-realisation, it is essential to cultivate an attitude of harmlessness. Ensuring that our actions do not create any suffering or hardship is important but harmlessness means something more than that. Rather than creating an ideal of causing no harm, the evolutionary path requires that our actions become beneficial – positive rather than merely neutral. To put it in a simple way, we should feel that we are doing our best to contribute to making the world a better place.

THE KARMA OF THE MIND

The action of the mind precedes almost everything we do and say and, because it operates unseen, it is the most overlooked. We can see what someone does and we can hear what they say but to know what they are thinking is a different matter. We can consider mental karma as the effect of our thinking, but it is far more than a matter of "bad" thoughts and "good" thoughts. Those are the tip of a very large iceberg indeed. Here we are talking about shaping our lives and, to a great extent, our destiny.

The mind is part of, and inextricable from, our energy field. As the mind changes, so does our energy. It is impossible to separate these two apparently different aspects of our being. Exponents of positive thinking know that if our habitual thinking patterns are positive, our vitality is generally better. How we think affects how we feel and, conversely, how we feel frequently affects our thinking. Our actions and words result from our thoughts and so, if we want to have some control over life, we need to take a grip on the mind. Unfortunately, because our minds run all over the place, making judgments, jumping from one thing to another and rarely remaining still enough to appreciate the present moment, we incessantly create a stream of karma. The effects created by our minds are chaotic unless we are focused.

When we think negatively, our whole energy field responds. If we feel angry about something, for example, blood pressure, heart rate, and breathing change as adrenalin is released into our body. Our emotions are fiery and our thinking is in turmoil. We think angry thoughts and all our happiness and natural kindness fly out of the window. Nobody likes to be near an angry person. It feels as though their energy is very spiky, keeping everyone at bay. So from angry thoughts, we reap the immediate effects of physical changes, unpleasant feelings, and likely create a barrier that makes others wary of us. If that is as far as it goes, the damage is relatively limited, but often words and actions come out of anger that can cause a chain reaction of problems. The karma of the mind can be very far-reaching indeed.

A consequence that is often ignored is the impact of thinking on our personal environment. We are surrounded by energy and we ourselves are like vortices of energy. As our energy changes, so does that of the immediate area around our bodies. Some traditions describe subtler forms of life that support the environment but which shy away or withdraw when there is violence or negativity. Whether we care to accept the possibility of that or not is not of great importance; we cannot deny that everything in us and around us is energy in one form or another and is therefore susceptible to strong influences. And perhaps we all experience those occasions when everything seems to go wrong, without any apparent logical cause – "one of those days". There is no superstitious suggestion here – just an invitation to consider the consequences when our own energy is incoherent.

Even when we are keeping our thoughts private, there is no escaping their results. One faculty of our minds is the ability to discriminate not only between one object and another but to evaluate qualities, which may be of objects, people, courses of action and even ideas. In fact, there is virtually no end to the power of the mind to discriminate. When we are evaluating, which is most of the time, there will always be a tendency to assess whether something is favourable to us or not. "This food is quite tasty but this is even better. I like this but I'm not so keen on that. It is raining and cold; therefore this is not a good day." We do it all the time. When we see something as good, our vitality temporarily lifts because at that moment we enjoy life just a little bit more. The blood vessels start to dilate and the energy of the body, sometimes called *chi*, flows much more easily. It would seem to make good sense, then, to evaluate things in a positive way to enhance our well-being.

The downside to this power of discrimination is that we can end up judging everything, and perhaps the most emotive and potentially damaging tendency of human beings is to judge other people. Being judgmental is one of the most difficult thought patterns to overcome, but we have to break the habit if we want to progress along our spiritual path. As soon as we entertain a negative thought, our energy goes out of balance. We create a spiral or loop that collapses inwards or implodes; we need to learn to do the opposite and radiate our energy. If we think for a moment in terms of light, whenever we think well of others and have kind thoughts, our radiance or light increases; but when we think badly of someone, it is as if a shadow comes over us.

How we think, and indeed what we think, affects every fibre of our being. Psychologists have always known that the mind can change our physical health as well as our emotional and spiritual health. It affects how we feel, how we behave and how we speak. It also conditions our future thoughts.

These are all incredibly important reasons for us to take care of our thinking, and with just a little effort we can, so that the organ grinder is in charge of the monkey once more.

Perpetual motion

We all think too much. If we try to stop the mind from having thoughts, we fail. Many people who begin to learn meditation give up because they erroneously believe that the mind should come to a complete stop when they close their eyes and leave them in some sort of mental void or oblivion. The ones who carry on and find inner peace are those who realise that the energy and activity of the mind have to be reined in gradually. There is no magic quick fix.

Not only do we think too much, there seems to be something in the modern psyche that convinces us that unless we are thinking, we are being idle. Few people can sit and do nothing unless they are having a nap. To sit without doing anything and without having thoughts is an enormous skill because, to do it properly, the mind must be absolutely clear. That requires extraordinary vitality in our mental faculty. But because we have not yet learnt how to do that and discover our inner potential, we generate a mental smokescreen of thoughts about – well, about anything really. Some people are very proud of the fact that they can multi-task, which to them means that they have the wonderful ability to think about three or four things simultaneously. Perhaps they can; or perhaps their thinking shifts from one thing to another in rapid succession without full awareness on any of them. But whether we claim to multi-task or not, what is certain is that our minds are in a state of almost perpetual motion. Even if we sit or lie down with the intention of doing nothing, the mind keeps working. Closing the eyes should help but we may find that as soon as our eyelids drop, the mind keeps going from one thing to another. In fact, it can be so alarming to discover the incessant activity of the mind that we may open the eyes again because we cannot relax. It's like going home for a bit of peace and quiet and finding instead that someone is watching the television in one room, there's a radio on in another and a lively conversation in a third. So we take the awareness outside again and look for something to do.

This *busy-ness* of the mind is not something imposed on us from outside, nor is it caused by some sort of virus or other affliction that we caught from someone else. Our incessant thinking patterns are self-generated; they are the result of mental karma – cause and effect. The more we think, the greater the movement of energy in the body and in the mind, resulting in even more mental activity. Every thought is preceded by a thought and is the cause of yet another. If we could harness all this movement and convert it into electricity, all the world's energy problems would be solved in one fell swoop. But we can't and so most of our mental energy is wasted. Our aim should not be to stop thinking altogether but to reduce our thinking so that the mind becomes clearer. When we achieve that, our mind becomes very strong because our mental energy is conserved. Just as importantly, as we begin to create less mental clutter, the body settles, too, and our sense of well-being improves.

Perhaps we could analogise the mind to a musical instrument. The more notes we play, the more we will want to continue playing; but the sounding of many notes doesn't necessarily make for a good melody. The musician has to exercise sufficient self-discipline to ensure his playing is coherent and has the right degree of harmony. He also has to know when to stop, otherwise there is a song without end. Our thinking is the same – it should be creative and harmonious, providing the basis for a positive and more enlightened mind, and also be capable of pausing for silence.

WHY WE HAVE NEGATIVE THOUGHTS

Even if we try to think positively, sometimes negative thoughts can still arise from time to time and it is easy to believe that we are failing or to feel guilty about them. It is very sad to hear someone refer to themselves as a "bad person", because of things that crop up uninvited in their mind, as though there is some inherent evil in them that sets them apart from the rest of humanity. Actually, we have already notched up a success when we notice that our thoughts have taken a negative turn; it's when we don't notice our negativity that there are problems. A thought is just a wave pattern of mental energy and a negative thought is one that causes our vitality to drop. We know that our mental energy affects our physical energy but negative thoughts have a way of sneaking up on us; and once that downturn in energy begins, we have to apply effort to reverse it to prevent it taking us over completely.

It helps enormously if we understand that every thought that passes through our mind has numerous causes. There is no need to go into any deep psychoanalysis about incidents in earlier life to understand there are various triggers that set the mind off in certain directions. The mind has its karma and to unravel all the chains of causation of everything we think would be an endless task, as well as a futile one. However, what is possible and what produces exceptionally fruitful results on our path of deepening awareness is to understand the fundamental causes, which exist in every human being.

Even at birth, there are already some patterns imprinted which affect our reactions to some degree. Some of these are from experiences in the womb, and others are from memory which may be inherited from our parents and ancestors through our DNA. Many cultures believe there are dormant memories from previous life experiences, too. It is upon these patterns that our future conditioning – education and all life's experiences – are built. As we develop through childhood into young adulthood, all manner of new patterns are retained in the storehouse of our minds.

Our interactions with others depend entirely on our self-perception. How we see ourselves colours our view of the world. If we are self-critical, for instance, and it is a rare person who isn't, we are likely to be critical of others, too. Our perception, whether of ourselves or of the world around us, is also deeply affected by what we believe; all illusionists rely on this. Yet the greatest illusionist is not some stage magician but our own conjuring mind. Due to the intricate programming or conditioning of our minds that has been going on since we came into this world, we tend to believe that what we see is real. We form conclusions about anything and everything that comes into our minds, based on a mishmash of preconceptions and beliefs, and, because of the law of cause and effect, we create endless streams of further thoughts. When we think negatively, it is simply that our minds are predisposed to judging and are conforming to patterns that we have already set up.

This tendency stems from a basis of *fundamental unenlightenment*. Unenlightenment begins as soon as we see ourselves as individuals – beings or entities separate and distinct from everything else. At whatever point in our primordial history it began, from it ensued a building up of a sense of "me", of "I am this but not that." This is very deeply ingrained in our psyche; and so we favour those things that we enjoy and which support this "me" and dislike or avoid those things we judge as unfavourable or even harmful to "me" or to what we have labelled "mine". The magician of the mind then has its way and a completely fabricated mirage of reality appears. We are the actors who have forgotten who we really are.

Unenlightenment is like a veil covering the eyes, whose fabric began as a single thread and which has been woven into something which entirely impedes our vision. Enlightenment is the reverse of this process and is often triggered by an event which causes our beliefs and preconceptions to be shattered.

BREAKING THE CHAINS OF CAUSATION

The beauty of the extraordinary capacity of the mind is that anything is possible. The mind is the cause of both happiness and unhappiness, and it is the latter that we are interested in eliminating. To do that, we have to break the innumerable chains in the mind that lead us into unhappy states. In spite of the title of this book, the Art of Not Doing cannot be acquired by doing absolutely nothing. Because the mind doesn't rest, if we do nothing at all the mind will fidget until we respond and do something. That's the manner in which the mind is used to getting its way. The Art is to learn to interrupt that process and to do the right thing at the right time, which on occasion may simply be to do nothing and be still.

Although we cannot undo what has happened in the past, the fact that we may think badly of ourselves or of others now does not prevent us from rapidly treading the path towards enlightenment. Negative trends of thought arise because of past thinking based on error; if we begin to correct the error, the chain of causation weakens and eventually breaks. It is like picking at the fabric of a veil and finding the thread which, when pulled, causes it all to fall apart.

The key is to take greater measure of our internal reactions by gradually re-educating the mind, changing the view that we have of ourselves and everything around us. Part of this is achieved by simply observing the reactions of the mind, thereby increasing our awareness. Once we become aware of thoughts and feelings, and the basis for them, the process of enlightenment really begins.

[3]

Self

WHO ARE YOU REALLY?

BEFORE YOU HAD A NAME, who were you? A name is just a sound – a call sign that we and others recognise. If we hear the sound of our name, our ears prick up and our attention is held – but we know we are not the name itself. Our parents or someone else may have given us our name but we were already here.

Apart from our name, most of us identify ourselves with the physical body. When we look at our reflection in a mirror, we may think we see ourselves staring back at us. But are we the body or just the face, and if the face, are we more the eyes or the nose? There is no answer to that because we cannot for sure even say what defines the body or any part of it. If the body is defined as the head, neck, torso, limbs, feet and hands, does the loss of one part mean the body no longer exists? Of course it doesn't, but that is the problem of identifying too closely with any form. When we analyse a little more deeply, we find that what we thought was the body is just a general term for a recognisable appearance. So although we may identify ourselves (and if ourselves, also others) by the body, we know that it isn't who we are.

The body grows into a largely pre-determined form. Inner intelligence instructs or informs the body's growth and its maintenance, principally through the programming of the DNA. For the body to work there also has to be energy or *chi*. Chi permeates every cell in our body, and indeed the entire cosmos. Without it there would be nothing – no drive, no action, no movement and no form. For us to appear and respond as human beings requires energy to collect or form as a cohesive pattern. This pattern is rather like a blueprint for the outer or physical body and is sometimes known as the "energy body".[6] How the energy body is affects our entire health and well-being. If it is out of balance because of an accumulation or stagnation of chi or depletion, sickness can result.

Like everything in the universe, the physical and energy bodies are subject to change and eventual demise. Nothing escapes the cosmic recycling plant. So these forms and appearances cannot be the self, the "me", we are trying to find. Of course, consciousness of the physical world is experienced through the medium of the physical body, its brain and its nervous system. But they are only tools or vehicles; they are not in themselves consciousness and are certainly not a "self" of any kind.

---

[6] Alternative descriptions are *vital body* and *etheric body*.

There are yet other aspects that we may refer to as "me". When we experience desires, sadness or any of the other countless emotions, from where do the feelings arise? They are not thoughts as such, nor are they physical sensations, although they can often give rise to both. We know that our level of vitality changes, as does the biochemistry that affects blood pressure, breathing, heart rate, perspiration and so on at the physical level. Our feelings are patterns of energy, more subtle than the vital energy or chi, and sometimes the term emotional body is used to refer to that aspect of our form or being in which they manifest. But are the feelings "me"?

When we walk into a room, something in us senses the energy that is present. If a room is cold or warm, we sense it through the mechanism of the physical body; if the energy of a room is stale or heavy, our vital or energy body responds to the lack of chi, as indeed it does to an abundance of it when we are in an invigorating environment. We can also sense a positive or negative atmosphere. If there have been sharp words, for example, we can often sense tension, and then we are also sensing through our emotional body.

Then there is our thinking faculty, usually associated with the brain, of which thinking is just one of many functions. But thoughts are much more than an activity of the grey matter in our skulls. Thoughts arise because of other thoughts, feelings, memory, experiences and beliefs and are a manifestation of energy. Thoughts affect the environment, not only through the words and actions that result from them but also because of the atmosphere they generate. In the same way that feelings can be said to arise in an emotional body, thoughts can be said to arise in a mental body.

Even though hidden from view, the subtle bodies – vital, emotional and mental – are really just different aspects of our form. In the same way that we can see a tree but not the energy that causes its appearance, we too have an underlying structure that functions at different levels. Our human world is full of millions of television and radio broadcasts, telephone messages and all manner of other communications that are invisible to the eye but are nevertheless endlessly present and without which life as we know it today could not be. Similarly, our own personal functioning is largely invisible. I cannot see "you" and you cannot see "me".

Apart from the structure of our form, both outer and inner, the personality by which we normally identify ourselves is an aggregation of perceptions, conditioning, thoughts, feelings, beliefs and patterns of reaction, all of which are embraced and experienced within our overall consciousness. None of these different aspects is permanent. Every single one is subject to a state of arising, a temporary passing and subsequent transformation. The play of these aggregates within our consciousness is sometimes referred to as mind. To find ourselves, then, we need to explore the nature of mind.

THE NATURE OF MIND

Finding the mind sounds a simple thing to do because it is with us all the time, after all. But pinning it down to any location is as impossible as it is to see the wind. Wind is totally invisible – all we can see and experience are its effects, not the wind itself. Wind is simply a descriptive term for air that is moving through the environment. We cannot see air or wind. Similarly, we experience the effects of the mind without being able to see it. So, what is the mind?

Most people would say that the mind is what they think with; some say it is the same thing as the brain; others say it is themselves. Certainly there is a common tendency to associate the mind with the head, because the brain is in effect the control centre for the body. Chinese philosophers associated the mind with the heart as much as the head and if we observe someone pointing to themselves ("this is me"), more often than not they point towards the heart rather than anywhere else.[7] Then again, if we say that the mind is not the brain but our thinking faculty, does that imply that mind ceases to be when there are no thoughts and that it doesn't actually reside anywhere?

We know that we use the brain in order to think and that it is possible to influence our experiences by tampering with the brain and its chemistry. The nervous system feeds into and reports to the brain by impulses of electricity. If

---

[7] Interestingly, they also regarded the gut as another location of mind, and Professor Michael Gershon of Columbia University in New York calls the gut "the second brain": Michael Gershon, *The Second Brain* (New York 1999).

the mind were the brain, then in deep, dreamless sleep the brain would have no job to do, but we know that it still carries out functions, regulating the body. A little deeper thinking may lead us to the inevitable conclusion that the brain cannot do what it does without some type of inner intelligence and most certainly not without the vitality that we call life. It is more than a lump of grey tissue with blood and electricity running through it. So the brain is the governor of the physical body as well as being the organ with which we experience thoughts. But it isn't the mind; it is a vehicle *for* the mind.

When we examine the nature of mind, very quickly we find that there is no single faculty but a collection of interacting and interdependent ones. The most apparent aspect is the thoughts that we experience almost incessantly. One thought yields another and it is difficult to say when one thought ends and another begins. A better description might be that we have streams of thinking and a rather apt term used in some Eastern teachings is *mindstream*. Our mindstreams are constantly changing, being influenced by the mindstreams of others. If we are influenced by something we read or hear, it is an effect on our mindstream by that of the writer or speaker. In turn, the writer or speaker will have been influenced by the mindstreams of others and, if we look deeply enough, we will find that there is no beginning and no end to these thought processes.

Perceptions are another aspect of mind. Every piece of information we take in through the senses is processed and interpreted. We know an elephant when we see one and that the sky is blue. Or at least, we think we do, but actually we rely on information we were trained with when we were young. Perception is labelling what we see, hear, taste, touch and smell. That labelling relies to a great extent on memory. If memory is lost through accident or illness, the patient often has to be taught many basic things all over again. If we cannot give a name to something, it belongs to the mysterious and the unknown. On holiday in a distant country, for instance, we may come across vegetables or fruit that are entirely strange to us. Our interpretive faculty can label what we see as something that has grown but beyond that we are stuck until someone explains to us what the strange objects are.

Perception isn't just about objects because we also label people, situations, weather – in fact, just about everything. We make assumptions and attribute qualities based on experience, memory and belief. Changing those perceptions, and the assumptions upon which they rely and arise, is a major factor in the process of enlightenment and requires some concentrated work. We will explore this further in chapter 5.

The "everyday" mind that operates in and around us is a collection of faculties. Sometimes we refer to it as the *thinking mind* to distinguish it from the more abstract qualities that arise as intuition and creativity. The thinking mind relies heavily on the ability to discriminate between one thing and another. It separates, classifies and catalogues. This is the intellectual aspect. The intuitive and creative aspect, on the other hand, does the opposite: it unites. The intuition sees the connectivity between things whereas the intellect looks for the differences. Both are important but it is the intellectual or discriminative faculty that generally receives more attention in our world. Education is based mainly on knowledge and intellectual skills, which are the drive behind business life, commerce and economic structure, rather than intuitive thinking and ethical or spiritual values.

The Art of Not Doing depends on balancing both aspects of mind. Thinking helps us to understand the mechanics of enlightenment; deepening our experience results from the awareness becoming clearer, so allowing the intuitive quality to surface. Not doing requires a quietening, and sometimes a complete cessation, of thoughts to allow the light of the higher mind to shine through. Higher mind is what may be described as the aspect of mind that deals with abstract thought. Ideas that seem to pop in from nowhere but make complete sense when analysed in the clear light of day come from this abstract area. Creativity depends on the influence of higher mind – unobstructed by discursive thought.

Through meditation, it is possible to access the higher mind – that which is beyond the everyday regions of our busy thinking. The experience changes with time, becoming refined, lighter and more meaningful. Deep insights can occur here and gradually a sense of wholeness grows – a sense of unity with the divine and all-that-is. By contacting this more profound side of our nature, life can change and become more complete. On the journey to discovering and establishing this changed reality, there are many interruptions and obstructions. Many of these arise from our emotions.

THE NATURE OF FEELINGS AND EMOTIONS

It is very difficult to separate the mind from the emotions. If we try to do it artificially, there is the danger of suppressing feelings, which in turn means we cause energy to stagnate in our system – for feelings are an expression of energy. A feeling that is sat upon is also a flow of energy that is blocked. Yet we want to attain a state of tranquillity which is undisturbed by desires, anxiety, jealousy, pride and so on.

Some schools of thought suggest that a strong person is one who dwells in the mental sphere rather than being beset by emotions. Although that may become a stage in our progress, reflecting a stable degree of clarity and stillness, to deny our true make-up and create a false or contrived persona is like building a house without proper foundations. It may look impressive but it won't last.

The Sanskrit term for mind is *manas* and desire is rendered as *kama* (not to be confused with karma). Most of the ancient teachings on meditation refer to something called *kama-manas* – "desire mind" – which is our thinking mind under the influence of desire and other emotions. Kama-manas is not a separate entity but an indication of the inevitable mixture of kama and manas. When we have a strong feeling, our thoughts tend to move in the same direction. It is extremely difficult to have a calm mind if we are feeling angry about something, for example. The play of kama-manas isn't all in one direction, either; our thoughts can easily stir up emotions, particularly when those thoughts are linked with memory, such as the thought of someone we have loved dearly and who is no longer with us.

Kama-manas is influenced by everything about us. If our energy is low due to physical causes, we may feel a little down and our thought patterns – our mindstream – will often reflect that. Our beliefs, which are really established thought patterns arising from all manner of conditioning, can instantly and often imperceptibly change the way we feel and think. Racism, war and most of the other problems in the human world stem from the play of kama-manas and from false beliefs. Perceptions, which are assumptions about what we see, hear, touch, smell and taste, cause feelings to arise and thoughts to flow.

In chapter 5, we will look at ways of dealing with emotions so that tranquillity can be enjoyed virtually all the time. For now, it is helpful to remember that our feelings are effects generated by preceding causes. They are temporary and surface due to numerous triggers; they also die down again. If we can remove the cause, the effect will not arise. As we are exceedingly complex creatures with countless "seeds" or causes within us that have been sown in the past, it is impossible to dig them all up, one by one. However, if we can deal with feelings so that their energy is released, and do this in an intelligent way so that we do not sow further seeds, we can re-establish an inner peace.

THE NATURE OF BEING

Disturbance to our natural peace comes from the machinations of the mind and emotions. If we transcend all thoughts and feelings, to arrive at a place of no thought and utter calmness, we come face to face with our own nature – Being. Being is not a condition, state or entity that is separate from us; it is us. It is the nature of everything. To know Being is not just a question of stilling our thoughts and feelings to reach a state of self-induced anaesthesia but to remain alert, with a quality of awareness that is extraordinarily clear. Some people mistakenly believe that "this is it" when they have simply attained a certain degree of tranquillity. This is like reaching the base station of Everest; the climb up the mountain is still to come. For our part, attaining a good measure of calmness is the first part of the process; gaining *insight* is the second.

Insight comes from sharpening the mind through both understanding and experience. Understanding demands at least some analysis. In other words, we have to understand something about our own nature. The knowledge we acquire usually comes from a variety of sources; much will be from our teacher, if we have one, or perhaps discussions with others and certainly from some reading. But all such imported knowledge is of limited value; real knowledge comes only when we know it for ourselves. The acquisition of insight may therefore mean some analytical meditation followed by looking into the mind itself. Over a period of time the light of the mind will increase and there will be occasional flashes of insight or knowing. It is a process that requires patience, an essential quality in our technological age of expecting instant results.

Being is beyond description because language inevitably has limitations and in any event the experience of Being changes as our own physical apparatus develops. If we are tired, for example, the enjoyment of clarity is difficult but as we grow in meditative experience, the nervous system becomes more refined and our state of consciousness likewise alters. However, it would be wrong to think that Being is a state of consciousness or even is consciousness itself. When we fall asleep, our loss of consciousness does not result in the annihilation of Being.[8]

Like space, Being simply is. It is the continuum in which everything occurs and appears. There is nothing that does not arise in Being and therefore nothing that is separate from it. Our limited perception is all that prevents us from seeing and realising our boundless nature. Realisation of Being is the immortality that sages have spoken of since time began, not permanent life in a physical body. To know Being is to know beyond the physical state, and indeed beyond the realm of thoughts and desires.

The importance and significance of learning the Art of Not Doing is to stop creating mental clouds that prevent us from seeing the sky-like nature of our own mind – its inherent boundlessness. When we know that our nature is clear and beyond any possibility of confinement, we have made progress in getting to know who we really are. The

---

[8] In fact, one of the experiences that can occur as we progress in meditation is the development of awareness in sleep.

progress that we must make is not like going along a road to a distant destination but is more like peeling away the layers of an onion. We don't have to go anywhere because there is nowhere to go; there is just something to find and that something is here, right now.

[4]

Presence

> *The past no longer is, the future has not yet come; the person who lives in the present moment lives in stability and freedom –* Gautama Buddha[9]

THE INCESSANT TRAFFIC of the mind is due, as we saw in chapter 2, to mental karma – the law of cause and effect operating in the mind. To reduce that flow and pacify the mind, in this and every instant we need to stop unnecessary thinking.

To understand the significance of the statement "the past no longer is" requires us to accept the present as it is, without any qualification. We cannot undo the past but we can choose how we approach the effects – the fruits of previous thoughts and actions. Regretting past acts and omis-

---

[9] See Thich Nhat Hanh, *Our Appointment with Life: The Sutra on Knowing the Better Way to Live Alone* (Berkeley, 1990).

sions is helpful only to the extent that we learn from our earlier errors so we do not repeat them. Once we have acknowledged them, we can offer them to God or the Universe and let them go.

"The past no longer is" is about not clinging to the past, good or bad. Nostalgia and guilt are very powerful forms of clinging that pull us backwards. Our attention gets drawn away from the only time there is – *now*. Thoughts about the past trouble us and cause us to daydream; they revive fears and unpleasant experiences, as well as pleasant ones. We regurgitate what should have been digested and eliminated long ago and, as a result, our perception of the present is coloured or tainted. Rather than seeing things as they are now, we superimpose memories and experiences of the past over them, like a photographic overlay.

Accepting the present as it is means letting go of the past in such a way that every turn of life is fresh. Imagine waking up after a good night's sleep and finding yourself somewhere different. Everywhere, there is something new to be discovered. This is how life should be – without having to move to a new bed every night, of course! Seeing whatever is in front of us, unclouded by the past, is like having a new beginning. Life becomes lighter, as though someone has taken away our heavy suitcases or rucksack and we don't have to bother with them ever again. Acceptance also means there is no "if only" – if only it wasn't raining, if only the colour was different, and so on; there can be no negativity if we accept things as they are, untainted by expectations we laid up in the past.

Now is incredibly precious. The present moment not only contains the fruits of the past – because current circumstances are the result of historical events – but it is also the instant in which we sow seeds for the future. Whatever we do now and however we react to life creates another link in the endless chain of cause and effect. Learning not to rake over the past and having the strength to trust that the future will be taken care of frees us from fear and worry. It also gives us the clarity of mind that is fundamental to the process of enlightenment.

MINDFULNESS – THE PRACTICE OF BRINGING OURSELVES INTO THE PRESENT

If we want to find inner peace, there is no option – we have to change the old habits of allowing the mind to lead us by the nose. If we think of the mind as being a useful piece of kit, like a special computer that has been given to us to help us through life, we can begin to use it rather than letting it use us. In the same way that it is easy to become a slave to a piece of technology instead of utilising it as a boon, we have ceased to be masters of our minds and emotions and instead are ruled by them. The practice of mindfulness reverses that trend and the beauty of it is that it is a fulfilling and enjoyable process. We don't have to become rigid or try to kill off our thoughts and feelings. On the contrary, we become more aware of them, but in a compassionate way so that we are kinder to life and life is kinder to us.

Mindfulness involves bringing our full awareness into everything. The initial task is to be fully aware of our actions by cultivating a still mind while walking, eating and so on – ordinary mundane actions that we normally do with only partial awareness. The reason we only do them with partial awareness is that many such actions have become almost automatic. We can do them without thinking and so we do. While the body performs the actions, the mind is free to depart elsewhere and concentrate on other matters, or perhaps just to drift into daydreaming. For instance, suppose we go for a walk to clear the head. While we're walking we think about all manner of things – problems at work, perhaps. Our mind is engaged with the thoughts but not the act of walking. Although physically we're walking, we do not know we're walking. We do not enjoy the experience of our feet making contact with the ground. Instead of kissing the earth, we pass by without noticing it. Thoughts simply create more thoughts and so the process goes on. When our walk is over, we may say that we enjoyed our walk and, indeed, we may feel better for the physical exercise. But did we really enjoy the walk itself?

The same principle applies to almost every activity that does not require our full concentration. The mind becomes divided – perhaps as little as 20% is engaged in what we're doing, and the remaining 80% is scattered. As mental processes use up energy, our physical energy becomes scattered too and as a result we become tired and less efficient. By appearing to do more, we actually achieve less. More importantly, we are inevitably unfulfilled and life is less than satisfactory. From a spiritual perspective, which is our main concern here, we are failing to establish a connection with our true nature. With mindfulness, we reconnect.

Establishing our presence through mindfulness is about taking charge of the mind and requires concentration. It also requires balance. If the concentration is too intense, it will lead to rigidity and a blinkered view; if it is too slack, distractions will lead us astray. If we think of mindfulness as being meditation in action, we can understand that the two basic faults in meditation – excitement and dullness – and their rectification, apply equally to mindfulness. We will look at these a little more in the context of meditation in chapter 6.

Our aim should be for steadiness, calmness and a relaxed state of alertness. Rather than being like rippled glass through which everything appears distorted, our minds need to become like clear crystal. In this clarity, we observe not only our actions but also our internal reactions. When a thought arises, for example, we should know that a thought has arisen and whether it is positive or negative. The same applies to feelings – we should be aware that this feeling or that feeling has arisen in us. Being aware in this way prevents us from being pulled by the undertow of our emotions and thoughts. We are in the driving seat rather than being driven.

Being an observer or a witness to what we are doing and experiencing enlivens our natural pure awareness. The effect is remarkably therapeutic. Pure awareness is stronger and lighter than our normal mental and emotional currents; it possesses inherent intelligence that is sometimes called "the light of the soul"[10]. It uplifts us and triggers a healing process; it is as though we become attuned to our own inner sound or vibration[11]. As mental clarity increases and emotions become more settled, we are able to place our full attention on whatever and whoever demands it. Listening fully and properly becomes a possibility; full enjoyment of our work, appreciation of our surroundings and love for others grow spontaneously and effortlessly. This is the magic of presence. All we have to do is cultivate it, and a key element to that is the breath.

BREATH – MORE THAN BREATHING

For thousands of years, it has been known that the breath is more than a physical action necessary for life; it also has a pivotal role to play in our spiritual development. Most of the time, we breathe unconsciously, noticing only when we have a desire for fresh air or when we simply cannot take in enough – and are literally out of breath – through exertion or respiratory problems. The physical need for oxygen from the air coupled with the need to expel carbon dioxide is something we are taught as children. In most cases, it is only later in life that we learn some of the remarkable effects that different methods of breathing can have on our vitality and on our spiritual well-being. The study of breathing is important in numerous disciplines and practices,

---

[10] Alice Bailey, *The Light of the Soul* (London, 1920).
[11] For more on the effects of vibration in healing the body, see Richard Gerber, *A Practical Guide to Vibrational Medicine* (New York 2001).

such as *pranayama* in the yogic tradition and *pre-birth and post-birth breathing* in t'ai chi and qigong.

In the cultivation of mindfulness, our concern is not with deep or other forms of breathing but with awareness of the act of breathing itself. The breath is like a bridge between the body and the mind. If the mind is agitated, the breathing tends to be shallower and faster and the body is in a state of increased tension. Conversely, we know from experience that when the mind is calm, the breath tends to be slower and smoother. If we can train ourselves to be aware of this rhythm, we begin to have greater awareness of our body and our emotional and mental reactions. It is a common technique to be aware of the breath during meditation but the development of mindfulness extends this practice into activity, which of course is more difficult because we have to engage the mind in actions as well as the breath. The rewards, however, are truly life-changing.

Awareness of breath acts like an anchor. An anchored boat stays where it is even if the wind is strong and the waves and currents of the sea are running wild. Without the anchor, the boat is tossed around and is prey to the whims of the sea. Our minds are very much like that. Without some form of stability, the mind is drawn into endless distractions and is subject to the surges of our emotions, which can often sow the seeds for unpleasant effects later on. They also waste precious energy. To cultivate the skill of the Art of Not Doing we must attain some calmness and stability and begin to master, at least to some degree, our minds and emotional responses.

In order to be effective, an anchor needs either to embed itself in something solid – the sea floor, for example – or to be sufficiently weighty to act as ballast. Similarly, our breath-awareness needs a firm base and the abdomen is ideal for this. Being aware of the gentle movement of the abdomen as we breathe is easy and has the effect of slowing the mind down and of centring the body's energy at the same time. Just the abdomen is good enough; if we want to refine it a little more, there is a focal point just below the navel that can be very helpful. It is traditionally said to be three finger-widths below the navel and just inside the body. In Chinese systems of health, it is known as the *lower dan tian* and by the Japanese as *hara*. The name isn't important. What is important is that we allow our awareness to rest there.

In meditation, we may begin by settling the mind with awareness of breath at the dan tian. Within minutes, the mind and body will become quieter and more settled. It is so easy. But what about in activity? The principle is much the same. The difference is that instead of putting our full awareness on the breath, we have a background awareness of it. It takes practice because the mind has been wild and erratic all our lives; and we will find that we have to keep returning to the breath over and over again. Making a habit of sitting quietly with the breath strengthens our practice; enjoying the rhythm of the breath while we undertake simple activity takes us to the next stage, and so we build it up. When we realise we have forgotten what we were doing, we just start again.

If we haven't yet developed the habit of breath-awareness, we need to kick-start it. Even if we are familiar with using the breath as a focus to develop mindfulness, it is valuable to refresh the focus fairly frequently.

It is a good idea to begin with a short period of sitting, say five to ten minutes, with the awareness just below the navel and feeling the rise and fall of the abdomen as we breathe.

Some people find it helpful to count silently with the breath – for example "1 and 2 and 3 and 4 and 5 and" on the in-breath and doing the same on the out-breath. Counting slowly helps induce calmness and can lengthen the breath slightly. Care has to be taken not to over-extend or tense up or even to try to reach the same number with every inhalation and exhalation. The body's requirement for breath varies and it is counter-productive to force the breath to be too slow or too long.

An alternative method to counting is to use mentally repeated phrases, thinking words such as "Breathing in" as we inhale, and "Breathing out" as we exhale. After a minute or two, this could be lengthened slightly to, "Breathing in, I am aware I am breathing in," and "Breathing out, I am aware I am breathing out." This is a very old, simple but very effective technique. Other phrases can be used – there is no prescription – so long as we know we are breathing.

Sitting practice has some wonderful benefits aside from getting us into a new habit. It has a very calming effect on both body and mind, making us feel better overall, reducing stress and strengthening the immune system. It is also central to mindfulness because if we can sit with breath-awareness, we are going to be able to enjoy practising in activity. To introduce mindfulness into actions, the easiest and best place to begin is with walking. To walk slowly and mindfully is like bringing heaven on Earth. With each step, we feel the ground with our feet, as though our feet are kissing or caressing the Earth; and as we continue placing one foot after the other, we breathe in and we breathe out. "Walking mindfully, I breathe in. With full awareness, I breathe out," or similar phrases can be useful here. Alternatively, at the beginning of our walk, we can count as we step – four, five or six steps as we breathe in and then count the steps as we breathe out – until a relaxed rhythm is established.

Once we are used to sitting and walking mindfully with the breath, our awareness should be more settled and clearer in other activity. We focus lightly on the breath while we are doing other things, allowing our breath to be with us. If a friend is with us, we don't forget she is there when we are reading or working; and when we pause our activity, we will smile at her. Treating the breath as our close friend is very helpful. When she is there, we have life and stability, the spirit of life itself and, when we are aware of her, there is great comfort and assurance. This is the way to generate presence.

BELLS OF MINDFULNESS

Mindfulness is very simple and the theory of it is easy to understand. However, it is not an intellectual exercise.

Mindfulness is an experience, a mode of living, acting and reacting. To live it, we have to change how we are, to go from a condition of mindlessness produced by tensions and distractions, to a state of simplicity. To have presence, we have to keep coming back to the present and, as we are very forgetful of the present, a system of reminders is very useful, if not essential.

The traditional method of remembering to return to the present moment is to have a bell sound at intervals. When the bell sounds, one comes back to breath-awareness. In communities where mindfulness is practiced together, a large bell is sounded and the whole community pauses for a few moments so that everyone comes back to the present. As most of us do not have the fortune to live in such a focused environment and have jobs, households and families to tend to, we have to devise our own system of remembering. A Tibetan singing bowl can make an excellent mindfulness bell. Every now and again, we can stop, sound the bell (or "invite it to sound", as is said in some Eastern traditions) and be still for a few moments, maintaining awareness of the breath as the sound gradually fades. If we use a computer or have a smartphone, there are programmes and applications that are designed specifically for this purpose and which sound a bell at intervals set by the user. We just have to remember to stop for a moment when we hear the bell.

When we are out and about, at work or in some other environment where the traditional method is not practicable, it is possible to use events in a similar way. If we are held up at traffic lights or are in a queue, for example, we can use that moment as a mindfulness bell. In fact, whenever our actions are frustrated, relax and bring the awareness onto the breath. Alternatively, we can think a sound, such as the syllable OM[12], in the mind, sounding it and letting it fade whilst we have our awareness on our breath. How often should we bring ourselves back in this way? As often as we need to is the brief answer but as a general guide, about every ten to fifteen minutes will be strengthening.

If we think we are too busy to use a mindfulness bell, then we probably need it more than anyone else. A very busy mind is usually too tense and we have to learn to release some of that tension. By pausing and mentally sounding OM, we are not using up much time – ten or twenty seconds – and to do that every ten minutes or so is possible for most people. In any event, we can cultivate the habit of coming back to the breath, over and over again. Each time we do so, there is a significant and beneficial effect on our energy.

ENERGY MATTERS

In our quest for peace, clarity and enlightenment, we cannot afford to ignore energy. If the energy of the body is free, if the body is aligned and the nervous system is in good

---

[12] The syllable is used as a mantra, or part of a mantra, in many Eastern meditative traditions and is said to represent the primordial sound of the universe. It is given here as a suggestion; any soothing sound could be used.

condition, our consciousness becomes clearer and easier. Many teachings on meditation stress the importance of keeping the body in good condition and maintaining a straight back when sitting for meditation, for example. We know from our own experience that if we do things that are not good for the body – maybe overworking, eating late or getting insufficient sleep – our consciousness becomes clouded or agitated.

This is partly to do with the nervous system and the brain but is also due to the fact that what we call the mind is a play of energy. In the Tibetan tradition, the movements of energy are called *winds*, a term which helps us to understand that if there is movement in one place, there is an effect in another. There are winds or subtle energy movements both in the body and in the mind. Movement in one causes movement in the other.

What does this have to do with mindfulness and presence? Two things:

Firstly, by practising mindfulness and continually bringing ourselves back to the breath and to the present moment, the mind becomes calmer and, as a result, the energy of the body changes so that we actually begin to feel better. The winds within the body flow more easily and there is less tension and less stress. Sleep improves as we become more settled within ourselves and our actions during the day are better focused and more effective. As the body becomes more comfortable, health tends to be better and, with the improved sense of well-being, the body becomes a more supportive vehicle for our consciousness. We work with the mind, which improves the body, and the body, in turn, supports the mind and consciousness. We have more physical and mental energy.

The second point is that with energy comes presence. We can only be fully present if our energy is also gathered and present. If someone is speaking to us, we can only listen properly if we offer the speaker our full presence. That means we are focused but also relaxed and receptive. Our consciousness is clear, we are connecting with the other person and with what they are wanting to communicate to us. The same principle applies to absolutely everything we do. We have to give our full presence to it – not by throwing every last drop of energy we have at the task in hand but by being relaxed and applying ourselves in a balanced way.

Balanced energy, a balanced life and presence all arise naturally from the practice of mindfulness. Then we hit the vital point – a happy, purpose-filled life.

[5]

Looking deeply

WHAT LOOKING DEEPLY REALLY MEANS

STILLNESS AND PRESENCE, once they begin to become established, enable us to take a deeper look at who we are and what our environment is. The approach we are going to use in this chapter is to examine everything we perceive through our senses, both inner and outer, so that we go beyond what first "strikes the eye".

From earliest childhood, we are trained to identify what we see, hear and feel by name. This has to be the case and always will be because without being able to label things, there would be no language and communication would be difficult if not impossible. This conditioning of naming everything is very sophisticated, so much so that when something cannot be described because of a lack of vocabulary, words are imported from another language or new ones created. The success of humanity to pin labels to things is remarkable but also a mixed blessing, the downside being that the mind has to work incessantly, sifting and cataloguing information. It then assigns a state of reality to whatever is described. For example, the words "my house" imply two fixed objects or entities – me and house – linked by a deemed relationship of ownership.

Our task now is to look beyond the outer and obvious, to allow the mind to transcend appearances and enjoy the serenity that will then naturally arise.

HOW TO LOOK DEEPLY AT OBJECTS

When we applied our minds to the subject of karma in chapter 2, we examined the principle of cause and effect in relation to states of mind and emotion. Every thought and every feeling has a predetermining cause. The same principle applies to what we see, hear, smell, taste and touch. Every object or set of circumstances that we observe is the end result of a multitude of causes, both previous and present. If we can learn to see things that way, our perception, and therefore our consciousness, changes. The objects or events are no different but our view and understanding change completely.

A good place to begin is to remind ourselves of some fundamental physics. Nothing that looks or feels solid is actually solid. All matter is composed of innumerable particles that are whizzing round in space. Even if we regarded the particles themselves as substantial, and quantum physics suggests they are not, they are minuscule compared to the space they occupy. The world of reality we see through our ordinary eyes is as much an illusion as are the moving pictures in a cinema film that look real but are intangible. If we put our hands out to touch the scenery or characters in the film, there is nothing there. Similarly, if we examine the appearances of our everyday world, what we thought was lasting and real is actually just a display of energy and particles. It is very impressive and the mind, of course, is easily impressed.

Aside from the amazing discoveries of quantum physics into the nature of matter and energy, there is a method of viewing things that requires no scientific understanding. Everything is simply a coming together of causes at a certain juncture of time and space. The causes themselves are extremely complex, going back almost into the realms of infinity, and it can be quite staggering to undertake a little analysis into the simplest and most mundane of objects.

Let's say we have an upright dining chair which is made of wood and has a padded seat. Fanciful though it may sound at first, it is not an overstatement to say that this ordinary piece of furniture contains the essence of the whole universe. If we take the trouble to look beyond the obvious, the boundaries to this little piece of solid matter start to dissolve. The chair doesn't dissolve, of course, but the vital key we have to understand and allow to sink into our minds without any shred of doubt, is that all boundaries are within the mind, not in the object of our perception.

To help transcend those mental boundaries, we start to examine causes. Let's assume for the sake of simplicity that the chair is handmade. The obvious contributing causes are that the chair was put together from a number of pieces of wood by a furniture maker and that he or she then put the padding on – some fibrous material, perhaps, covered with a piece of textile and held in place with staples or studs. If we try to trace the timber back to its source, though, we inevitably find there is no originating point. The tree from which it came was comprised of many elements – chemical elements in the ordinary sense, biological factors such as species and seed, and elements in the wider sense, such as warmth, soil, moisture, and so on. The tree contained the earth, water, heat or fire, air and space. Take away any single contributing cause and the tree simply would not have come to be – and, of course, no tree means there can be no chair.

Each of these elements relies on the existence of the earth, the sun and the rest of the solar system – and, if we continue those chains of causation, the galaxy and the universe. There is no end to the long line of preceding causes and effects that result in the wood. The same applies to every other material used in the construction of our chair. So when we look at the chair, instead of seeing just a chair, we can see that it is also trees, rain, light, the sun and all the other factors.

That is a wonderful way to start the habit of looking deeply. We need to go further, though. If we examine the human elements that resulted in the chair, there are other endless chains to be found.

We can begin with the physical aspects of the human angle. The carpenter or joiner has a body that is continually changing and requires the circulation of physical constituents – respiration, food, liquid, warmth and elimination. All those factors have no beginning or end. Remove any ancestor and there would be no chair. Then there are the conditions that provided the education and training, intelligence and creativity that resulted in the design. The ambit spreads wider as we embrace the cultural influences that have led to the production, and indeed bringing to market, of the chair.

Although we can never reach the origin of any object, contemplating in this way is extraordinarily freeing for the mind. If we meditate well on our chosen object of analysis, we might come to the conclusion that there is no object after all. Instead, we have a set of circumstances or conditions that are manifesting or taking on a particular appearance at this juncture of time and space. There is nothing to be grasped, nothing to become emotionally attached to. The object will one day take on a different set of appearances as its supporting conditions wane or change. If it were taken to pieces and all the parts laid out on the floor, without anything being taken away, the chair would no longer be a chair. The chair could be discarded, burnt, or it might rot. The only thing to have disappeared is our perception of a form we give a certain name to. Nothing has gone; it has simply changed.

Instead of something that has been manufactured or created, we might choose for our analysis a naturally occurring object such as a pebble or a flower. We can go through the same process of contemplating its origins, or rather the contributing factors that have led to its appearance. Analysing something in this way begins to release the mind from its habitual tendency to see everything as real or established. It is best and most helpful to do this quite often until we become used to the idea of seeing beyond the apparent. Even then we need to contemplate in this way every now and again in order to refresh our view and avoid returning to old habits of thinking.

HOW TO LOOK DEEPLY AT OURSELVES

If an inanimate object has a deeply complex history, the make-up of a human being might seem beyond any possible consideration. In spite of the human tendency to judge our fellows and their innumerable faults and idiosyncrasies, judgments are always wrong because no-one can really know someone else. From the point of view of enlightenment or spiritual progress, there is only one human being that we can and should start to examine and that, naturally, is oneself. So how can we go about it without embarking on a long and perilous journey of self-indulgence? After all, isn't there a danger of seeing "me" as extremely important and interesting and not being concerned about anyone else?

On the contrary, if we do it correctly, and it isn't difficult to do so, the opposite will be the case. As we see ourselves more truly, the ego and selfishness begin to fade. Enlightenment is synonymous with liberation – freedom from basic ignorance of who we are and from the innumerable attachments and aversions that stem from that. Free of these, it is said the light of pure knowledge will purify and inform our consciousness, influencing everything we think, say and do.

To investigate ourselves well, we must have a methodology and the simplest and most effective approach is to work from the outside – our physical appearance and attributes – first. It is quite possible to approach the other way – from an investigation into the nature of mind – but for that we need to have good and stable meditative experience to begin with. If we are fortunate enough to have developed that stability, we can tackle things in whichever order we choose. For now, let's look at it in logical sequence.

Our starting point, then, is the body. We can consider the body in the same way that we looked at objects. The contributing factors include our parents and ancestors, and the physical elements arising from food, water, heat and light, our DNA and so on. We also need to look at the body in terms of its changing nature – from the time of conception until the present time – and its inevitable future demise. To have a clear sense of the impermanent nature of the body is of paramount importance and to undertake a graphic contemplation of the dying process can play a very powerful part in achieving that. More than that, we can look a little more deeply by seeing that the body we have now was in fact never born. There is no single thing that can be identified as the body. It has constituent parts that are constantly changing and even conception and the growth of the embryo are not beginning points – they are conditions which have or had their preceding conditions. The body we have now is not the same as the body that came out of our mother's womb; it has evolved from it but is not the same, just as a tree is not the same as the seedling it once was. Our present body was not born but is an appearance resulting from preceding and current conditions. This is a point that we really need to meditate on quite deeply.

When the time of what we call death comes, the body will not be the same as it is at this minute. Some prefer to say that it is the body that dies rather than the person, in an acknowledgment that consciousness and the body are not the same. The subject of death is a very profound one, too deep to go into at this point. For our current purpose, it is enough to contemplate the temporary nature of the body and the fact that at death the elements of our physical appearance and structure do not cease to exist – they change into other things, whether that is through rotting in the ground, cremation or some other process. The body and its constituent parts are merely recycled.

What is the point of contemplating like this? Done well, it releases very powerfully much of the tension that comes from the excessive attachment (and sometimes aversion) we have to the body so that we become more in tune with our *psychic energy*. The psychic energy can also be called the energy of the soul – the dynamism and creativity of our spiritual nature – which can have significant effects on how we feel and how we respond to life.

After looking at the impermanence of the body – our outer form, we need to turn our focus inwards. Examining the non-birth and non-death of the body naturally evolves into an examination of aspects of ourselves that impinge on our consciousness. We are constantly besieged by feelings and thoughts, which we may regard as part and parcel of our character, and the same principle of non-birth and non-death applies to those too. If we feel a dislike for one particular person and fondness for another, for instance, currents of mental and emotional energy are being triggered by numerous factors that are different in each case. Although these factors are usually quite complex, there is no need to go into a searching psychoanalysis in order to release the tensions that they cause. We would never come to the end of all our idiosyncrasies and their causes; we could even end up creating new psychoses as we uncovered them. However, we need to do something otherwise our mental clarity will continue to be affected by them and our journey of gradual enlightenment will make little progress.

The first thing we need to do is to cultivate a general but very definite understanding that thoughts and feelings are impermanent. They arise when certain conditions are present and not at other times. As the conditions change, so do our internal reactions. It is wrong to think that we are an unhappy person or an angry, jealous, proud or lustful one. There can be no such thing as a permanent fixture of anger or jealousy anywhere in the universe. This why it is totally wrong to think we have failings that can never change. Patterns of thoughts and emotions cloud our awareness from time to time but, like clouds, they are ephemeral and appear on the wind, disappearing by the same means. If we have thoughts of a negative nature, that is to say thoughts that could produce harmful effects if carried out as either action or speech, they do not turn us into a "bad person" any more than a dark cloud renders the sky into a bad one. The sky itself doesn't change, nor does our fundamental pure awareness. The difficulty we often create for ourselves is to see these thoughts as real and allow ourselves to be dominated or influenced by them. If we cultivate the habit of seeing all thoughts and feelings as impermanent, they will release their hold on us.

The second thing we must do is to recognise thoughts and feelings as they arise. The tendency is not to do that but to drift along with the mental and emotional currents. We need to break that tendency because, as we saw in chapter 2, every reaction is the seed or cause for further effects. So we need to train ourselves to observe. Becoming an observer detaches us from the immediate effects of *kama-manas*, the combination of desire and other feelings and the thought processes triggered by them. Acknowledgment and identification are the key factors in observation. If, for example, we feel a little irritable, before any harm can come of it we identify it: "a feeling of irritability has arisen in me". Then we feel the feeling, noticing its effects. Remaining peaceful, the observer observes. Sometimes gradually and sometimes quite quickly, the feeling will subside because we are not feeding it. It is released in the positive space of our awareness. We prevent the causation of further discomfort, the sowing of seeds of future negative karma. It is essential that we don't try to judge how or why the feeling has arisen because that may set off other unhelpful thoughts and emotions. Acknowledging and observing fully is enough. In this way, the clarity of our awareness and our mental faculties will steadily grow.

The same principle of observing applies to thoughts. "A critical thought has arisen in me," for instance. Although it is a thought, there will almost certainly be a feeling associated with it, so we should notice that too. Getting into the habit of observing our thoughts without judging them will start to slow down our mental traffic. Most of us have congested minds and freeing up mental space allows our thinking processes to be clearer and of better quality. In our task of looking deeply at ourselves, we will develop increasing understanding of our own nature.

Deeper than thoughts and emotions are our beliefs and habits that structure and influence the way we think and behave. Although these may seem entrenched in us, they also share the quality of impermanence. It is vital at some stage to examine these ingrained patterns of thought that programme many of our reactions. Beliefs that have been with us for a long time can be, and often are, transmuted as a result of acquiring new information. Some are very useful, and indeed necessary, but if a belief causes us to think or act in ways that are harmful or that are selfish, we need to purify it by exposing it to the light of pure awareness – "the light of the soul". When we know that we are reacting in a certain way because of what we believe, we should observe that reaction and the belief that is driving it. This releases energy held in by tension and sheds a little light in the mind. For example, we may decide to engage in an exercise regime to make us fitter and healthier – but might there also an underlying belief that as a result we will also look better and be more attractive? Or we may have lost our phone or camera and suspect it has been stolen by a nearby youth who is looking "shifty" – until we find the missing item where we had left it (and then the young person doesn't look shifty anymore). How we relate to others depends very much on what we believe about them. Perhaps, too, we are driven by political and religious motives or by ingrained superstition. Closely related to beliefs are habitual patterns of thought and reaction. Habitual tendencies are not necessarily harmful but it pays to observe them. When the mind is lucid, habits do not govern us but are seen for what they are.

Looking deeply at ourselves should lead us to the conclusion that we are not our body, our feelings, our thoughts or even the characters that we present to the world. We are something far more profound that is neither born nor dies. There is a boundless and timeless aspect to our nature that is both empty and full at the same time. It is a mystery because it cannot be described in words – it can only be experienced. That experience can only come when we learn to stop.

HOW TO LOOK DEEPLY AT OTHERS

There is no difference between you and me, not really. It is only the charade we put up – the masquerade of the personality – that makes us think we are separate and unalike.

When we see another person, it is easy to see them just as a person – an individual whom we think we know well, slightly or maybe not at all. If the person we know well acts out of character, becomes unexpectedly ill, dies or suffers some type of trauma, we may be shocked or upset because the picture of them we hold in our minds is contradicted or even shattered. A mental image we have of a friend is only that – an image based on perception, presumption and imagination. The image we have of others usually cloaks them with a degree of permanence. Rarely, if ever, do we think of others as ever-changing manifestations of innumerable factors. If we haven't seen someone for a number of years, it can be startling to see how they have aged, for example in growing up or growing old. We are forced to create a new image that has to supersede the one that has occupied our memory until now. There is no fault in this because it is normal human behaviour; but our perception arises from a mistaken or unenlightened view.

For those we know barely or not at all, a different symptom can arise that also comes from an unenlightened viewpoint. Here, the effect can be a negative one. We may not particularly like them – or for the majority of the population, whom we cannot possibly know, we may have a neutral attitude. Yet if we look deeply enough, we will see that those we don't know are no different in their ultimate nature to those we profess to know well. Somehow or other we need to equalise our contradictory views of our fellow human beings, otherwise all our perceptions, thoughts, reactions, speech and behaviour will be based in ignorance.

How should we look at others, then? Firstly, as we have already discussed, we have to correct our self-perception. By investigating our own nature, we create the foundation for seeing others in a different or new light. If we can see the impermanent and vulnerable nature of the persona we present to the world, the limited self, we know that what we see in others is a limited view of their real nature. The other person we see is an appearance in time and space with thoughts, beliefs and prejudices generated by the conditioning that life has given them. Beyond these quirks of character, though, their boundlessness is the same as our boundlessness. Their idiosyncrasies, like our own, are a veneer that hides their inner nature. Our task is to recognise what is truly there, which is indivisible and not subject to the limitations of a personal separate self. Until we are sufficiently enlightened to see others in that way, we must train the mind to view our fellow human beings with compassion and equanimity.

The second stage is to see that others are fallible and vulnerable, just like us. Every human being seeks happiness and fulfilment. If we look deeply enough, we will see that even in complete strangers. Then we will find that the tendency to judge others starts to deflate. Labels previously used to define people are no longer valid. That is a very good thing because immediately we sow the seeds for peacefulness and generate less mental karma. When we observe someone else doing something we regard as wrong, we have to remind ourselves that all wrong actions are based on mistaken perceptions. If the other person were enlightened, their actions would be right no matter what we thought of them. Because enlightenment corrects all perception, an enlightened individual does not make mistakes. On the other hand, if the other person is living under the cloud of ignorance and acting in accordance with their deluded beliefs, just like us and the majority of humanity, it is rather like the pot calling the kettle black if we judge them. All we do is reinforce our own prejudice and water the seeds of conflict that lie within us, as they do within every unenlightened human being. So, we do not judge.

The third stage, which strengthens us immeasurably and hastens us along our evolutionary path, is to see others as ourselves. To do this, we must realise that everything we see, animate or inanimate, is like a reflection arising in our consciousness. Our consciousness receives signals via the senses and displays a picture. If we regard the mind as a sense, as the Buddhists do, we can understand that the conditioning in the mind gives us signals in addition to those arising through the consciousness of the eyes, ears and other senses. For example, if we see a person at a distance who looks like our friend, we may mistake her as a friend. Until we know for sure that she is not a friend, we may be convinced that she is. Our consciousness sees our friend, not a stranger. As a result of that conviction, feelings appropriate to our friendship will arise, unless or until we discover we were mistaken and then warmth may be replaced by disappointment or embarrassment. The other person, of course, is quite innocent in this and doesn't change at all.

Seeing others as ourselves is to realise that there is no such thing as friend or stranger but a reflection of life appearing within our minds. We see a cloud because of conditions that cause water vapour in the atmosphere to be visible to the human eye. Similarly, we have appeared as a result of conditions and, like the cloud, are birthless and deathless. Only our physical appearance comes and goes. The same applies to every human being. Whether a person is a friend, enemy or complete stranger makes no difference to the truth of their nature, which is the same as ours. So although it may seem a little strange at first, we will gradually find it completely natural and liberating to imagine the person we are observing or listening to is us. In the beginning, we may only be able to sustain this perception for moments at a time, but with perseverance it will build up. Then a strange thing happens – we listen more closely, we empathise, we feel compassion and our understanding grows. Ignorance and delusion evaporate like fog in the morning sun. How wonderful!

LOOKING DEEPLY AT CIRCUMSTANCES

One day things are going swimmingly and another everything seems to go wrong. Sometimes mundane activity can fill weeks and then suddenly something momentous happens, which might be good or bad. Some people's lives appear to be filled with good fortune and others are not so lucky. What life deals us is a matter of chance or fate. Or is it?

As we saw in chapter 2, all circumstances are effects coming together – causes coming to fruition at a juncture of time and space. They are the result of a multiplicity of actions, of karma, a subject which is almost unfathomable in its complexity. If we lead a life of tranquillity, we create fewer causes that will later disturb our equanimity, but even a person who lives serenely can find events happening out of the blue. Sometimes we can see the immediate causes, such as the breaking of a plate being caused by lack of coordination brought on by tiredness. Often, though, it may seem that we are caught up in something that has nothing to do with us or that we are victims of bad luck.

There are two things we need to do to deepen our understanding of events. The first is to develop the skill of accepting that in the present moment everything is as it is. This doesn't mean resorting to fatalism where we see ourselves at the mercy of the whims of the universe but just accepting that right now life is how it is. That is easier to say than do, so we need to look inwardly at this point to notice whether there is any resentment or other negative feeling in us. If there is, it is a clear indication that we are not accepting the moment. This helps to cultivate the observing nature of our awareness. Actually, the observer is present all the time but our thoughts, beliefs and emotions cloud it, like marks on a window obscuring the view. It is generally wrong to suppress our thoughts and feelings, though, because what is really required is retraining of the mind. Once we learn to see and think differently, the emotions become less troublesome. So we train ourselves in learning to ac-

92 | *Andrew George Marshall*

cept and observe and to react only when there is a need to do so. To do that, we have to convince the mind that that is the right and logical thing to do.

The second approach to adopt is to see events for what they really are. In the same way that we learn to look at ourselves, others and objects in a deeper and more understanding way, we must do the same with events. That requires seeing both the current circumstances and the causes that led to them as having the qualities of impermanence and interdependence. Impermanence means that circumstances are not fixed and inevitably will change. When we watch a beautiful sunset, it can be so stunning that we want to capture that moment; but we know it hasn't been there long and indeed is transforming before our eyes, only to die within minutes of it having appeared. Or maybe there is a storm with high winds and heavy rain; but it hasn't always been there and the gales and lashing rain soon pass. The sun, of course, doesn't set; it just appears to do so and the storm is an aggregate of climatic conditions coming together. None of these phenomena is permanent and each depends on other causes to appear or be present.

The same applies to all events in life. Many may be caused, at least in part, by human actions rather than nature but if we look beneath the surface, beyond the apparent, we will see that every circumstance is transient and ephemeral.

KNOWER, KNOWING AND THE KNOWN – A LESSON IN UNITY

When we look at an object, there is a trinity – the observer, the observed and the process of observing. If any of the three is missing, there is no observation. The same goes for knowledge; there has to be knower and known, linked by knowing. There is no listener without that which is listened to and the act of listening. Throughout history, deep questions have been posed by philosophers about this relationship. Is there a sound if there is no hearer? Is there an object if there is no seer? These, and questions like them, are about consciousness and are directly relevant to our understanding if we wish to master the Art of Not Doing. Looking deeply involves investigating the trinity of relationships and transcending them to experience pure knowledge and unity of consciousness.

It isn't necessary to embark on a lengthy intellectual analysis but rather to engage in looking at ourselves by becoming still. When we have attained a good degree of mental stillness, it becomes possible to lift our awareness higher and then we may have a clear experience of consciousness, knowing that there are no boundaries, just a unity of extraordinary purity. At that point in meditation, knower, known and the process of knowing become one – or rather the apparent separateness of them dissolves. That experience and the knowledge it gives is the aim of meditation, which continues until it is so firmly rooted in our awareness that it remains with us at all times. Our consciousness is then invincible and life is filled with joyousness and bliss.

[6]

Meditation

GRASP THE NETTLE – MEDITATE!

IT DOESN'T MATTER WHETHER we are complete novices at it, have been doing it for years or have never done it before – we need to embrace the practice of regular meditation if we are to master the Art of Not Doing.

We are all beginners at meditation because every time we sit to do it, it is a new session and it is important we arrive at our meditation seat with a fresh mind. The method we use will vary from time to time but, whatever the technique, the aim is to know ourselves and we can only do that if we have an attitude of wanting to discover and to learn. So we should always begin with a degree of enthusiasm, which helps the mind to focus and encourages us to enjoy the practice. We should also know the reason why we are meditating. If we are aiming for tranquillity, for instance, it is not the right time to be carrying out analysis of some issue or to be working on the flow of energy in the central channel (which we will discuss later in this chapter).

Millions of people practise meditation simply because it makes them feel better – helping to calm the mind, reducing stress levels and often improving health. Simple meditation techniques enrich life by reducing mental chatter so that the quality of the present moment is appreciated more deeply. Many meditators report improved personal relationships, increased creativity and productivity in their work and other activities. In short, meditation enhances life and results in growing happiness.

But there is more. Enlightenment is the cultivation of consciousness which is totally free of any experience of separateness, where the sense of "I" dissolves into unity, and where all boundaries are seen to be false and nonexistent. It is accompanied by all-encompassing love and compassion and what can only be described as *knowingness* – a supercharged intuitive state where anything can be known. This is both the flowering and fruition of the Art of Not Doing.

Meditation has to be more than relaxing in a chair or sitting on a meditation cushion, pleasant and helpful though that may be at times. Relaxation is part of the meditation process but there also has to be focus and it is the nature of that focus that is crucial. Different times and circumstances will warrant the use of various techniques, but in essence there are three approaches that need to be employed.

The first is to pacify the mind. If the mind is tranquil, we can make much progress. The mind is rather like the sea or a lake. When the water is in turmoil, it is impossible to see below the surface or, even if we can see something, what is seen is distorted. If it is still and clear, though, we can see into the depths. We can only know ourselves when the mind is calm. The second approach is sometimes called *insight*. Insight requires looking and that has two main phases: analysis and observing. The third approach, but no less important than the other two, is the development of love and compassion – the heart qualities.

TRANQUILLITY

It is a common misconception that meditation is spending time with a blank mind. When we are stressed and the mind is agitated, it would be wonderful to be able to flick a switch and turn everything off. But we all know from our own experience that that rarely happens. Because incessant mental chatter is uncomfortable, the remedy that most of us use is to look for a distraction. We are probably conditioned like that from childhood because the usual method for stopping a child from crying is to divert its attention. If we are unhappy, we generally look for something else to engage us, unless the misery is so strong that we remain immersed in it. This doesn't really achieve anything, of course, and is rather like turning the car radio up loud so that we can't hear the rattling from some mechanical fault.

In meditation, we find that there are all sorts of "mechanical noises" – endless streams of thoughts that lead onto even more streams. Unless we do something about it, our period of sitting will be little more than a glorified daydream. That is not to say that thoughts are wrong, but we need to treat them correctly. Initially, we may use awareness of breath or a mantra in order to reach some stability in meditation. Eventually, however, we will reach the stage where we are able to be aware of thoughts and feelings as they arise. It is at this point that we may begin to observe thoughts and, as soon as we observe them, find that they instantly dissolve. Through this and similar techniques, an increasing state of tranquillity will arise in our meditation and we may experience increasingly longer periods that are apparently free from thought.

INSIGHT

The development of insight has two principal phases. The first involves extensive analysis so that we understand, without any doubt whatsoever, that the model of reality with which we have been conditioned all our lives is totally false. We have to investigate the impermanence of all appearances, including ourselves. This follows the line of looking deeply as we discussed in chapter 5. It is easy to think that we do not need to do this because it is all so easy to understand. However, unless we do this over and over again, we will not reach the indefatigable point of understanding and will sink back into old habits of thinking. After a long period of contemplating in this way, we can begin to look more deeply at our own mind. We should try to locate the mind and examine its qualities, including size, colour and so on. Of course, we will not find it but unless we carry out a thorough investigation, we will not experience for ourselves that this is the case. We need to persist in this and be patient.

The second phase of developing insight is to look deeply at the mind. This is a point where analysis is no longer necessary – we just gaze into the mind, as though consciousness were looking at itself. Enlightenment is not a process of increasing our intellectual understanding so much as increasing our awareness by broadening our horizons until we have a new experience of reality. The inward gazing has to be carried out with equal balance of yin and yang[13]. That means that we must be alert so that the mind doesn't drift into dullness and yet be peaceful so that there is no excitement of thoughts. For this reason, it is essential to be well-practised in attaining and maintaining a state of tranquillity.

It is important that we have guidance from someone who is experienced in these types of meditation because it is easy to become stuck or discouraged and we need some sort of feedback on how we are doing.

HEART MEDITATIONS

Whereas tranquillity meditation works on the mind and, indirectly but very effectively, on the body, insight meditation is concerned principally with the mind and with consciousness. The combination of these will eventually give us

---

[13] Yin and yang: a Chinese term for opposite qualities, which can be applied to both physical and mental states. Harmony is said to arise when there is proper balance of opposites. This concept is examined in more detail in chapter 7.

great vision and understanding but we also have to cultivate the qualities of the heart – love and compassion – so that we become very warm human beings. We need the fire of the heart as well as the light of wisdom.

Enlightenment involves the development of our whole being, not just the mind. In order to experience the deeper aspects of insight, our vital energy has to be raised so that our brain and nervous system resonate at a much finer frequency. It is easy to neglect the body when we are dealing with the mind but both are important and affect each other. By altering our mental focus, we change the energy that runs through our body. One of the most effective means of doing this and supporting our meditations and mindfulness practice is to generate loving kindness and compassion.[14]

The essence of heart meditations is to visualise others and to deepen the love or warmth that we feel for them; for those for whom we feel nothing in particular – complete strangers, for example – we imagine that we know them very well and so cultivate some feeling that can then be deepened. Gradually, we develop this so that we have a desire to alleviate the suffering of all people and, indeed, of all sentient beings. This work needs to be done carefully and with enthusiasm, ensuring that we avoid the pitfall of becoming blasé in our practice.

---

[14] For an examination of this subject in greater length, see: Andrew Marshall, *Awakening Heart: The Blissful Path to Self-Realisation*, (Stafford 2011).

One might wonder whether heart meditations are superior in some way to those that develop insight, or vice versa. Should we give one type preference over the other? The short answer is that both are necessary, once we have attained some level of tranquillity. Unless we have a teacher who guides us otherwise, it is a good idea to alternate them so that we work with one aspect for, say, a week and then the other for a week. Or, if we meditate twice a day, we may prefer to practise one meditation in the morning and the other in the evening. There is no hard and fast rule and we must do what works best for each of us.

ENERGY AND THE CENTRAL CHANNEL

Although meditation is primarily about the mind, energy within our body plays a very significant part. It is difficult to have a clear experience when we are feeling sluggish or, at the other extreme, excited or agitated. In meditation, the mind needs to follow a middle course, neither falling into drowsiness and daydreaming nor chasing the wild geese of distraction and emotions. The mind and energy work together, reflecting each other. If our energy is clear, light and settled, meditation will be easy; conversely, if our mind is in a state of excitement, our energy will be disturbed and then it will be difficult to settle or to concentrate.

Throughout the body is a complete network of energy pathways. Because these cannot be observed by orthodox means – you will not find them no matter how good a microscope you have – they are often regarded as being part of an energy body that underlies, permeates and informs the physical body. The acupuncturist and other practitioners know that when there is congestion in any of the energy pathways known as *meridians*, pain or illness can result. The clearer our meridians and smaller energy channels are, the better we feel and the more effective we are. The mind is clearer and we are generally more energetic – we have more vitality.

Looking after both mind and energy is of inestimable importance and in the next chapter we will look at the practical things we can do out of meditation that can positively affect our experience in it. For now, it would be helpful to consider a major principle in meditation practice: the flow of energy up the central channel.

The central channel is a major energy pathway that runs, as the name suggests, up the centre of the body. It is not a physical pathway so, like the meridians in acupuncture and other energy disciplines, it will not be found by dissecting the body. It is part of the subtle body structure that includes the energy body or vital body, as it is sometimes called. The channel starts at the perineum and goes up through the core of the body to the crown.[15]

When energy makes its way up the central channel, it will go only as far as our nervous system and consciousness can accept. Just as our eyes need to adapt to bright light

[15] It is related to, but not the same as, *sushumna*, a path that energy is said in traditional yoga teachings to travel, from the base of the spine to the top of the head; nevertheless, there is some correspondence as the rising of energy directly affects experience in the meditator. There is much reference to the central channel in the tantric teachings of Tibetan Buddhism.

when we come out of a dim room into bright sunshine, our whole system has to acclimatise to this energy slowly. There is no point in rushing the process any more than anything is to be gained by pulling on a sprout emerging from a seed to make it grow faster. However, like the sprout, growth can be encouraged by providing the right conditions. There are two things in particular that we can do.

First, and paramount, is to cultivate our natural kindness. Kindness and generosity, together with love and compassion, are qualities of the heart centre, which can draw the energy upwards in a very safe, natural and practical way. Working with energy is not a question of some sort of spiritual technology but of application of principles to life. So although meditation on loving kindness is an essential aspect of growth, the heart qualities only establish themselves through daily life, away from our meditation seat when we are interacting with others.

Being aware of the central channel is the second. Sometimes we may visualise a thin column of light running up the core of the body to the crown. A few seconds now and again is enough. If we are aware of the central channel, it is easier for the energy to flow along it when it is ready to do so. Alternatively, we can simply be aware that there is energy running through the core of our body. Awareness affects energy flow and a gentle, relaxed awareness of the channel, without intense concentration (which will tend to cause congestion rather than a flow), can help with mental clarity in both meditation and activity.

INNER REALMS: NOTHINGNESS AND THE FORMLESS

When we experience quietness during meditation, it is important to guard against falling into the trap of self-delusion. From time to time it is possible to see colours or unusual sights or to hear sounds of various sorts. On occasion there can be surges of energy. At other times it may seem that we have come to a stage of "no thought" and we may believe that some immortal state has been attained. There is a danger we may think we are having a significant experience, when almost certainly we are not. Experiences come and go; they are ephemeral and, although they can seem amazing to us, they are no more significant spiritually than the appearance of a snowflake or a rainbow, beautiful as these are. Most meditators find that their meditations are predominantly quite ordinary and mundane but feel extremely good and clear when they rise from their sitting and go into activity. That is probably the better way to be.

Traditionally, there are said to be three main areas or realms of consciousness in which there is experience of one sort or another and which are below the threshold of what might be called an *enlightened state*. An enlightened state is one where the experience is of unity and where any sense of being an individual with a separate or permanent self has dissolved. Even though we may cross that threshold from time to time in our meditations, it takes many, many years before such a state becomes established. Until then, our minds will venture in the three realms of *desire*, *form* and *formlessness*.

In the *desire realm*, there is much mental activity and the attention is pulled this way and that by feelings, memories and countless thoughts. There may be many appearances or images playing like a movie on the screen of our mind. The form realm is much more settled and refined. It is much lighter and altogether happier. Within the *form realm*, there are said to be many layers or strata in which increasingly refined states of consciousness may be experienced, often as colours or light. Although there is some stability in the form realms, eventually everything changes. Beyond form, the *formless realm* is more subtle and very difficult to describe. There is nothing to see, nothing to hear, nothing to experience – except formlessness. As with the form realm, according to tradition there are different levels of experience.

In both the form and the formless realms it is possible to have an interlude of no thought. We may find ourselves in a state of "nothingness" and it is at this point that some people believe they have reached a stage of perfect meditation. We have to be very careful of that because such belief prevents further progress. Believing we have "made it", motivation to attain transcendence or *samadhi* weakens. In true samadhi, the experience of self disappears but there is no loss of consciousness. In formlessness, with the experience of no thought there is still the awareness of being the meditator or observer. In samadhi, observer, observed and the observation are one and the same, non-differentiable.

MONKEYS AND ELEPHANTS – THE RELEASE OF KARMA

In chapter 2, we considered the law of cause and effect. Difficulties in life come from the working out of seeds of karma sown in earlier times. Causes give rise to effects; how we react to them causes future effects, positive or negative. The most significant type of karma is of the mental kind because our beliefs, thoughts and reactions are the most powerful forces in our lives. There is also emotional and physical karma, resulting principally from memories stored in our system. Memory of something painful, for instance, may cause us to flinch under certain circumstances, even though we may have no conscious recollection of the original pain.

Unless there has been a physical injury, tension in the body generally has mental or emotional causes. In other words, tension in the mind creates tension in the body. Meditation generates ease on all levels. Simply from sitting, we dissolve stress. Life takes on a rosier hue and our reactions to life in general are far more positive. By meditating, we create positive karma because it helps us to sow seeds of positivity and it also dissolves many of the negative ones that were sown in the past.

When we meditate, we start to clear out much of the clutter that is stored within us. As we become more tranquil, the body relaxes deeply and many tensions, some of them very old, are released. Like monkeys that have become bored with spectators who have no more food for them, they move on and we are freed from their chattering and pestering.

As we progress with our meditations, we will come across feelings and thoughts that seem to rise up from the deep. They can be so strong that they bar the way until we do something about them. These are the elephants. Often we will have no idea where they came from and trying to analyse their source can evoke memories that are not helpful – they just churn up more thoughts. The key to dealing with strong thoughts and feelings is to neutralise them and we do that by observing them with the light of consciousness, as we considered in chapter 5. If a feeling is present, we observe the feeling and feel it. It helps to identify it, saying to ourselves "a feeling of anger has arisen in me". In other words, we label the feeling but we don't judge it. If we judge our thoughts and feelings, particularly if we feel badly about having them, we make them stronger rather than help them to dissolve. Instead, we view them impartially and they begin to lose their grip. It takes time but, if we are patient, the old elephant that has been sleeping eventually gets to its feet and lumbers off, never to be seen again.

PRACTICE[16]

There is a time and a place for everything, it is said, and meditation is no exception. If there is some structure and discipline, our meditation will bear fruit. The mind has had a lifetime of wandering and needs help in being retrained.

---

[16] See Appendix for two suggested meditations.

The environment has an effect on us; if our meditation place is cluttered, we are less likely to sit down in a focused frame of mind. So the place of meditation is important – structure of space – and we also need to have some discipline of time, both duration and time of day. Structure and discipline may seem old-fashioned and there are some who say they have no place today – that we can meditate whenever we like and for as long or short a time as we wish. Of course, we have freedom of choice but in the same way that we will not get a good grounding in a subject without study and application, a loose approach to meditation will not get us very far either. If we want to fill a pot with water, the pot needs to be sound and not riddled with holes or cracks. Similarly, for progress in meditation, our practice needs to be strong.

To understand how and why meditation works is relatively easy, but the Art of Not Doing is not achieved merely by intellectual understanding. Paradoxically, it requires us to do something. What we need to do is to get on with it – day in, day out. That means sitting down in a suitable place and meditating for whatever time we have decided. Preferably, the place should be quiet and uncluttered and if we can use the same place each day, so much the better. If circumstances mean we have to use somewhere else, we should be strong and flexible enough not to mind. Whenever possible, we should meditate about the same time each day. Some people meditate just once a day, which is fine, but if we can manage two sessions, we will gain even greater benefit. Sitting for meditation at around the same time brings our practice into our daily rhythm; that helps us to be ready to do it and the regularity strengthens the meditation because our body's energy is more settled.

The length of each session should be determined before we begin, otherwise our meditation may become woolly and we will drift. Some traditions advocate quite long sessions but that advice isn't practicable for people leading busy lives. It is better to do a short meditation, say 10, 15 or 20 minutes, that is focused and that we can fit into our routine without too much adjustment, than to attempt to carry on for an hour that we can only manage now and again. In any event, a long meditation is more likely to result in dullness or drifting.

Associated with structure is the posture that we adopt. Not everyone can manage to sit in a traditional cross-legged position, let alone in full lotus. If we are using a chair, it is important to ensure that our back is kept straight. If the spine is perpendicular, or nearly so, meditation will be clearer. Some chairs encourage us to recline and that is not good because the body's energy flows differently and the experience can tend towards drowsiness. Sitting with the back unsupported is often advised. This is good provided we do not end up focusing on aching back muscles or feeling generally uncomfortable. The most important thing is to sit in a position in which we are comfortable – relaxed but totally alert.

Focus

During the meditation itself, it is essential to maintain focus. The mind, out of habit, will tend to wander. The key to maintaining focus is to have balance. There are, in essence, two opposing poles and the trick is to find the midway point. One pole is *dullness*. Dullness comes as a result of the mind becoming too yin. In this state, there is a lack of energy. We may drift into daydreaming or just feel rather sleepy. In either event, not much is happening. The other extreme, the yang pole, is the presence of too much *excitement*. The mind is too lively and jumps about from one thought to another. It is not wrong, in fact it is perfectly natural, to experience either dullness or excitement. The trick is to turn these states to our advantage by being aware of their presence. In a sense, we become like the proverbial fly on the wall and observe what is going on in the mind. As soon as we realise there is dullness coming, we should lift the awareness – it may help to adjust our posture or to look upwards for a few moments. If the dullness is so strong that we cannot overcome it, it may be better just to rest as good meditation is unlikely to come. Excitement can be remedied in a number of ways. Looking at thoughts as soon as they arise should help or we may need just to bring our attention to the breath. If these fail, looking at a fixed point on a wall or the floor in front of us for a minute or two should resolve the matter.

Rather than dwell on these two extremes, however, the real blessing in meditation is to find the midway point between dullness and excitement and to maintain our focus on that. At first, we may only be able to keep that up for short periods but with practice we will be able to maintain it for longer and longer. Even if we are meditating for insight or to develop love and compassion, it is good practice to spend a few minutes first reaching a state of tranquillity.

POST MEDITATION

Meditation is really the preparation time for our activity so when we emerge from our meditation, we should take care to come out slowly, to rise from our seat happily and calmly and gradually go into activity with complete mindfulness. The time between meditation sessions is called the *post-meditation period* and it is as important, if not more so, than the meditation itself. It is the time when we should be developing mindfulness and presence, as we looked at in chapter 4, and if we have been developing insight or the heart qualities, the post-meditation period is all-important for stabilising those in our consciousness. In the next chapter, we will look at this more deeply.

[7]

Balance

HARMONISING YIN AND YANG

Yin inward, yang outward; yin heavy, yang light; yin cool, yang warm; yin slow, yang fast. There is no yin without yang and no yang without yin. Each is contained within the other and yet if we search, we can find neither – Anon

THE ART OF NOT DOING is learning the skill of balancing yin and yang, internally as well as in outer life. In a state of perfect balance, there is no movement – *wuji*[17] – where yin and yang are perfectly blended. As soon as there is movement, there is *taiji* – the operation of opposites. In life's dealings, there is always the interaction of the two, like the working of one leg and then the other to provide both power to the wheels of a bicycle and balance to its rider. When we are thinking, there is movement in the mind and there-

---

[17] *Wuji* is often translated as "boundlessness" or "infinity".

fore the play of opposites takes place in the mind, which can also move out into our body's energy system. Behind the thinking there is the indwelling observer, what some would call the self, which is totally still and in a state of wuji. Like wuji, the self is not contained but by its very nature is boundless.

BALANCING THE OUTER

Harmonising yin and yang on the outside for our purposes is balancing the body, our surroundings and our activity. Because our minds are still fixed in duality – this and that, me and other, good and bad, and so on – outer conditions influence the mind and our consciousness. If we are suffering physically, it is difficult to have a clear mind; a busy and noisy environment can be disturbing, and the quality of our activity both affects and is affected by our inner state.

Caring for the body should be relatively straightforward. The right balance of diet, exercise, suitable environment and sleep should help to keep us in good health. But the body is more than a physical structure and we need to care for and nurture the energy system that underlies and informs the physical too. In terms of diet, if we consume too much, particularly if the food is heavy, sweet or oily, the body and our metabolism can become too yin; conversely, an over-reliance on raw or spicy food, for example, may make the body too yang. The subject can become very complex as there can be localised imbalances and what is right for one person's constitution may quite wrong for someone else's. The more we are in touch with our own nature, with our inner stillness, the easier it should be to balance our diet and, by and large, our intuition will guide us. Often, we just have to listen to what the body is telling us.

The correct level and type of exercise will support a balanced life. As with diet, what is right for one person may be wrong for another but there are certain factors that are common to most. One is that the younger we are, the more exercise the body needs. As we age, the amount and extent of aerobic exercise should be moderated. Unless we are sick, we all need some exercise and, as with anything, it should not be taken (or reduced) to extremes. A modern tendency is to sit too much and then try to make up for it now and again by being very active – taking up running or dance exercise classes, for instance. That takes the body from a yin condition to one where there is an over-application of yang – one imbalance is replaced by another.

Moderate exercise is always better and some forms, such as t'ai chi or yoga, are designed to stimulate and nourish the energy system as well as giving the body adequate movement. The Indian sage Bodhidharma[18] is attributed with introducing Buddhism to China and with it the practice of meditation. He is also said to have taught certain types of qigong[19] exercise because practitioners were sitting for hours on end without any exercise. This was making their bodies too yin and their experiences in meditation

---

[18] There is a mixture of historical fact and legend about Bodhidharma, who lived around the turn of the 5th and 6th centuries CE.

[19] Sometimes written *chi kung* – to work with energy.

were becoming dull. As qigong works on the energy of the body as well as providing physical movement, both meditations and bodily health improved. Powerful aerobic activity may revitalise us but carries the risk of creating imbalance whereas the beauty of disciplines such as qigong, tai chi and yoga is that they balance our energy as well as giving a zing to life.

Our environment may not always be of our choosing but everything we take in through the senses is processed and interpreted. In addition, the prevailing energy in the environment can influence our own energy-field and affect the way we think, feel and act. If we have a choice of environment, it makes sense to choose one that makes us feel calm and refreshed and inspires us. That is the ideal. If we live and work in a busy town or city, some time in the countryside or in a park as often as we can is time well spent. There is another aspect to life that we may not think of as environment but which has as much if not more impact than the area in which we live. This relates to our personal life and preferences – what we read, how we mix with others, what programmes we watch, how we use computers, phones and other means of communication, what we absorb from the media and elsewhere – all of these have a huge impact on our consciousness. Most of us get lost in these from time to time and their significance is not just their quality but their speed and sheer quantity. The Art of Not Doing is about making the mind less busy. All information we take in is processed internally, which requires energy and attention and often creates busy-ness. The mind is overstimulated and becomes too yang.

It is crucial to reduce this overload of input, otherwise we will never enjoy clarity of mind. The information environment is a jumble of energy. Information is given and received by the communication of energy, or rather patterns of energy. The atmosphere in a library is very different from that in a supermarket, and not just because of the lighting and sounds; what is stored on the shelves has a very different quality of energy. We can be affected by surroundings in two particular ways: one is through being open or receptive to the prevailing atmosphere; the other is by engaging directly with it – through books in the case of the library, or taking in the forms, colours and written information on the packaging in the case of a supermarket. What we can learn from this, apart from minimising contact with certain types of environment as much as practical, is that we are directly affected by the quality of what we surround ourselves with, whether at home or at our place of work or study. It isn't necessary to lead a monastic life to master the Art of Not Doing – far from it – but we do need to be selective in both the quality and quantity of visual, auditory and electronic data. This will help enormously in attaining inner and outer balance.

BALANCING THE INNER

The balance of yin and yang in our consciousness is of supreme importance. There are two aspects of consciousness that are of relevance to us here – inner and innermost. Inner is what is generally termed "the mind". It is our day-to-day awareness which thinks, feels, believes, is happy, sad or angry and which controls our actions, our omissions and our speech. Innermost is deeper than the inner and is the observer that is always present. It is the core of our being around which everything revolves.

The inner aspect of consciousness – mind – has been our main concern so far because we cannot know the innermost while our mind is pulled this way and that. Through the practice of mindfulness, which we looked at in chapter 4, the mind becomes less agitated and we can then begin to gain some deeper insight into our own nature, as we discussed in the last two chapters. When we were considering meditation, we touched on the need to find a balance between the two extremes: sluggishness or dullness on the one hand and excitement or agitation on the other – yin and yang. In the post-meditation periods, it is crucial that we try to maintain the same balance, swinging neither one way nor the other. If we feel sluggishness, a little stimulus is probably needed, unless we are tired, in which case rest or sleep is the obvious and natural remedy. Often, all that is needed is a change of view or some physical activity. At other times, we may notice that the mind is too busy, maybe a little tense, and is either easily distracted, jumping from one thing to another, or is burning with emotion on an endless train of thought. Unless we apply an antidote, the thoughts will continue to run, and cause havoc, until we reach a point of exhaustion. This is an example of excess yang leading to an inevitable yin state, the classic yo-yo or seesaw syndrome. The remedy for the yo-yo is surprisingly simple: we observe our thoughts and feelings dispassionately.

BALANCING THE INNERMOST

The innermost is the eternal observer in us. The observer is impartial, not judging anything, but with the capacity to know everything. From the observer the intuition flows into our minds; into the observer, all experience is absorbed. The nature of this innermost aspect of us is boundless and therefore its reality is beyond yin and yang or, put another way, all opposites are reconciled and united in it. It is wuji but plays out in taiji.[20]

The innermost itself cannot be restricted but what the observer experiences is limited by the restrictions we place on it through the gateway of the mind. The observing nature has the potential of unlimited intelligence; the extent to which that intelligence is utilised depends on what is put before it. Our minds – our thought processes, beliefs, perceptions and habitual tendencies – haven't caught up with our innermost reality yet. They have to grow into it and the key to doing that is *alignment*.

Alignment of our minds with our intrinsic nature is of paramount importance to our spiritual growth. If we are

---

[20] According to Chinese Taoist teachings, *wuji* is an infinite state where yin and yang are perfectly balanced. As such, there is no movement and no form, no positive and negative, no light and dark, nothing to be seen; and yet the potential for everything is there. The faintest impulse or flutter means the opposites have again come into play and *taiji*, the interaction of yin and yang, emerges.

concerned with ourselves and our own happiness above all else, there is an absence of alignment and we suffer from spiritual imbalance. The observer is in effect held down by our blinkered view of life. What has this to do with yin and yang? The mundane and the personal is heavy compared to the spiritual; when our main concern is ourselves, our view is too yin. On the other hand, if we neglected the mundane and concentrated only on spiritual matters, our view can become too yang. In this context, yin may be regarded as the "lower" pole and yang as the "upper". In Taoist philosophy, man or woman is between Heaven and Earth. It is the same premise. We have to be balanced between upper (Heaven) and lower (Earth). The more common imbalance is too much concentration on personal affairs and desires but it is possible to go too far the other way and not "have one's feet on the ground".

The importance is this: if we are spiritually balanced, we are aligned with the flow of evolution – the flow of life. The remarkable and creative intelligence of the innermost can reach and inform our thinking. Our experience of life changes as we see a wider view. Can the observer or innermost be disturbed? No, but it becomes hidden when our mind is pulled this way and that by strong currents of thought. The observer, which is serenity itself, does not go anywhere. When we come back to the present moment, we re-establish the connection between outer, inner and innermost. We are flooded with clear awareness, which is our natural state. Then we can focus on the middle way, the steadfast path, and the sublime energy of what is sometimes called the inner self will lead us to a true state of joy-ousness.

BECOMING THE OBSERVER

Now we are nearing the end of this book, our journey has almost begun. It is time for us to begin the process of becoming and living who and what we really are. It is a mistake to think we are the innermost, the sacred, and distinct from the body and the life that surrounds us. We are all of it. If we think that the outer is separate in some way from the inner, we are still living in the world of this self and that self, of me and everything else. We are the innermost, the inner and the outer, all at the same time. The peel of an apple is as much apple as the flesh and the core. All is just apple. And we know from our earlier discussion on analysis and interdependence, in chapter 5, that the apple is tree, earth, sun, rain and everything else. In fact, the apple is a manifestation of the essence of the entire universe. We, too, are the manifestation or appearance of essence. We may not know what that essence is – that discovery is a joy yet to come. So if we think, "I am really a divine being and this body is like a spacesuit that I occupy temporarily while I learn some important lessons on this planet," that reinforces the idea of separateness, of the profane being something different from the sacred, or of the light being able to exist without the dark. We have to progress beyond that limited way of thinking and realise the unity of absolutely everything.

To embrace the Art of Not Doing is to embrace the whole of life. It is to become the observer and the observed, engaged in the bliss of enlightened observation. We have to develop skill in this and also strength. Sometimes we will lose our balance and feel everything is lost. There will be periods when mindfulness is hard to recover because the currents of life, both inner and outer, seem to rob us of our tranquillity. At other times, everything seems to flow more easily. Like any other art that is acquired over time, there has to be perseverance as well as inspiration. When things are easy, we may not be making as much progress as when we face obstacles, which can strengthen us. It is important to remember this.

Over time, greater mental clarity will inevitably develop. The unity of observer, observed and observation is realised when the mind is settled and clear, when our vitality is good and our focus is pure and undistracted. When we walk, we know we are walking, aware of every step; and we know also that we are breathing, aware of every in-breath and every out-breath. When we are preparing a meal or carrying out a task, we know that we are in the right place at the right time and doing the right thing in the right way. We also know when to stop, in the full confidence that there are times when the best thing is to refrain from doing anything, from saying anything and perhaps from even thinking anything. Just to be and to be in silence is often the most productive thing we can do.

We can begin the Art of Not Doing right now. There is no need to wait for a better day because now is the best day of all. We don't have to leave it until we have some free time because the observer is timeless – beyond time and beyond restriction. The observer is always free. It is not the observer that creates endless chains of cause and effect – those are the products of minds with a limited and mistaken view of reality. It may not be possible to sit down and meditate at this very moment but we can bring our full awareness and presence into every second.

That is the key point – to be in touch with our own essence or spirit. Then we enter the stream of life, where our own inner evolution can unfold, and our natural potential can blossom. Life becomes as it should be: peaceful and happy. No stress and no contrivance. All we have to do is learn to stop, to breathe and to appreciate the present. It's so simple. And so amazing!

Appendix

MEDITATION 1: TRANQUILLITY OR "CALM ABIDING"

If you are not familiar with meditation, ensure you are seated in a comfortable position – the back straight, hands resting in the lap or on the thighs, and the tip of the tongue lightly touching the hard palate, just behind the top front teeth. If sitting in a chair with the feet on the floor, allow the legs to be uncrossed. If you prefer to sit on the floor in a crossed-leg posture, a cushion under the bottom can help the posture.

Close the eyes[21]. Allow yourself to smile a little – this helps relaxation – and be aware of the body and your posture.

Begin to notice the rhythm of your breath. Don't try to breathe in any special way – just observe the rhythm.

Gradually lower your attention to the abdomen, to the area of the navel, still noticing the rhythm of the breath. Stay with this for 5 or 10 minutes.

---

[21] Although it is possible to meditate with the eyes slightly open and with a downward gaze, most people who practise meditation do so with the eyes closed because it brings the attention inwards more easily.

Then listen and be aware of what is going on in the mind. Has the mind come to a state of quietness or is it distracted? Is remaining in this meditation easy or is there an urge to go back into activity, some restlessness? Do we feel happy and content or are there emotions stirring?

As thoughts, feelings and perceptions arise in meditation, simply observe them without judgment. Notice how they dissolve.

Continue observing your internal reactions for several more minutes.

When you are ready to come out of meditation, do so slowly. Feel your own natural quietness. Feel the quietness of the space around you. Gradually introduce a little movement in the body, starting with the hands and feet, and then perhaps stretching the arms or legs very lightly. When you feel ready, gently open the eyes and sit for a few more moments before going into any activity.

Note: it is better to begin with a short meditation, say fifteen minutes, that is fairly clear than to sit for a long period, which may result in drowsiness or dullness.

Meditation 2: Looking Deeply

Sit in a meditation posture (see above meditation) and close the eyes. Ensure the mind is settled and calm. If there is any agitation, sit with awareness of the breath until quietness is restored.

Begin by contemplating the impermanence of your body: think how it has continually changed since you were a child, and will carry on changing. Consider the various factors that have resulted in its be-

ing here today: your parents and endless line of ancestors, the physical elements of heat, moisture, air, solidity, as well as the chemical elements, that all support its structure in time and space, and innumerable other causes that you may think of in your meditation. Realise that when you look in a mirror, what you see isn't the real you but the reflection of an appearance with a beginningless and endless history of cause and effect. Even when we die, the body will not cease to be but will change into other elements.

Consider how your mind is shaped by memories, experiences, education, input of information, hopes and aspirations and maybe sometimes by fear. Reflect, too, how patterns of thinking are influenced by beliefs and perceptions. None of these factors has any permanence; like clouds that move across the sky, they all change and are replaced. Like the sky, the mind is the emptiness of space in which everything appears.

Look a little deeper. Where is the mind? Does it have shape or colour? For that matter, where is your self? Where is that which we call "I" and "me"? Keep looking for your mind and your self. Instead of locating them, eventually you will discover that your true nature is boundless. But you have to find this for yourself and experience it for yourself. This will take time and many meditations.

When you come to a point in your meditation where there is nowhere else to look, just gaze inwardly, smile and relax. Sit quietly for a while longer before bringing yourself out of meditation slowly.

Thanks to...

Huge thanks to all those who have encouraged me to keep writing, especially to Gloria, my beloved wife and best friend, and to Claire Wingfield, whose editorial skills have kept me on track when my sentences have crossed the line of intelligibility.

My deepest gratitude goes to the long line of selfless men and women – the sages of the human race – who, since time immemorial, have passed on the wisdom of life from generation to generation.

About the Author

Andrew George Marshall leads courses and workshops on meditation and mindful living, and has done so for over twenty years; he also teaches taiji and qigong. He is the author of two other books – *The Great Little Book of Happiness* and *Awakening Heart*, which are available in both print and ebook editions – as well as numerous articles. Andrew lives and works in Staffordshire, England.

If you have enjoyed this book, please let others know. And, if you can spare a few moments, a short review would be greatly appreciated. Thank you!

Andrew's website is:
www.joyousness.org.uk

...and there is a website for this book:
www.theartofnotdoing.com

Collected articles are available at:
www.fieryheart.org

Index

Printed in Great Britain
by Amazon